Whiteness in Puerto Rico

Whiteness in Puerto Rico

Translation at a Loss

Guillermo Rebollo Gil

BLOOMSBURY ACADEMIC
LONDON • NEW YORK • OXFORD • NEW DELHI • SYDNEY

BLOOMSBURY ACADEMIC
Bloomsbury Publishing Plc
50 Bedford Square, London, WC1B 3DP, UK
1385 Broadway, New York, NY 10018, USA
29 Earlsfort Terrace, Dublin 2, Ireland

BLOOMSBURY, BLOOMSBURY ACADEMIC and the Diana logo are trademarks of Bloomsbury
Publishing Plc

First published in Great Britain 2023
Paperback edition published 2025

Series design by Adriana Brioso
Cover image © Ryan Bonneau/Alamy Stock Photo

A catalogue record for this book is available from the British Library.

Library of Congress Cataloging-in-Publication Data
Names: Rebollo-Gil, Guillermo, 1979– author.
Title: Whiteness in Puerto Rico : translation at a loss / Guillermo Rebollo Gil.
Description: London ; New York : Bloomsbury Academic, 2023. |
Includes bibliographical references. | Summary: "The issue of race in Puerto Rico has, historically
and institutionally, been presented as a non-issue, with the majority of Puerto Ricans identifying
as white in the US census. As a result, pervasive racial discrimination against Afro-Puerto Ricans
has largely been, and continues to be, left unattended. In this book Guillermo R. Gil examines the
social construction of whiteness on the island, using the study of American racism to inform his
analysis of Puerto Rican racism and the two culturally distinct, yet intrinsically linked, spaces to
study whiteness. Examining the work of Puerto Rican activists, writers and artists, Gil documents
the ways in which whiteness shapes and informs Puerto Rican cultural producers while
simultaneously being challenged by them. Cross-disciplinary in approach, Notes on Whiteness
in Puerto Rico speaks to the present political moment in a country marked by austerity, disaster
capitalism and protest"– Provided by publisher.
Identifiers: LCCN 2022056549 (print) | LCCN 2022056550 (ebook) |
ISBN 9780755635504 (hardback) | ISBN 9780755635542 (paperback) |
ISBN 9780755635511 (epub) | ISBN 9780755635528 (pdf) | ISBN 9780755635535
Subjects: LCSH: White people–Race identity–Puerto Rico. | White privilege
(Social structure)–Puerto Rico. | Racism–Puerto Rico. | Puerto Rico–Race relations.
Classification: LCC F1983.W48 2023 (print) | LCC F1983.W48 2023 (ebook) |
DDC 305.80097295–dc23/eng/20230207
LC record available at https://lccn.loc.gov/2022056549
LC ebook record available at https://lccn.loc.gov/2022056550

ISBN: HB: 978-0-7556-3550-4
PB: 978-0-7556-3554-2
ePDF: 978-0-7556-3552-8
eBook: 978-0-7556-3551-1

Typeset by Newgen KnowledgeWorks Pvt. Ltd., Chennai, India

To find out more about our authors and books visit www.bloomsbury.com
and sign up for our newsletters.

Contents

Acknowledgments

The author would like to thank the editors of the following publications, where sections of this text first appeared: *Latin American and Caribbean Ethnic Studies, CENTRO Journal, Dead Skunk* Magazine, *Understanding & Dismantling Privilege*, and the *Lunch Break Zine*.

1

A Noose

The woman is neither white nor Black. She's grey, with blue undertones. Or blue, with grey ones. It's hard to tell. The woman I'm attempting to describe is in a painting by Carlos Dávila Rinaldi. The painting is entitled *Hijos de María* (Sons of María). There's two of them: the baby in her arms and the boy standing to her left, holding on to her hip. He looks as if he's bracing himself for something. They're in the airport, presumably because they are about to join the more than 200,000 islanders who left Puerto Rico in the days, weeks, and short months after Hurricane María made landfall on September 20, 2017, as a category 4 hurricane (Schachter and Bruce 2020).

The woman's expression is of contained despair. Containment here looks like a moving mix of dignity and valor. You know she has everything to lose because her children are with her. You know that, probability-wise, they will face substantial hardship wherever they land stateside. But, though weary, her figure does not communicate fear so much as resolve. A decision has been made, and regardless of whether it will allow the family to flourish, María has the wherewithal to see it through.

The piece is part of Dávila Rinaldi's 2018 *Aftermath* show in the Plaza las Americas shopping mall in San Juan, a ten-painting exhibition focusing on the iconography of those first few weeks and months after the disaster. Gas tanks, gas stations, and the long lines of people waiting to buy gas feature prominently. *Hijos de María* stands out for its setting, but also because it's the closest the artist comes to portraiture. The rest of his figures are flattened out, cartoon-like, more insinuations of a type than renderings of actual people.

Consider *The Venus of Octane*, for example. She appears with her back to the viewer, in tight fitting jean shorts, a too-short yellow crop top, pink curlers in her hair. Actually, there's no discernible hair; it's all curlers. There's a small tattoo on the back of her neck. It resembles a marihuana plant. She's carrying two red gas tanks and a red cell phone. Her fingernails are painted red, as is the entire backdrop. As such, the painting does not register like a depiction of scarcity or hardship. If it weren't for the gas tanks, she could easily be in line at a store or for a concert. To be honest, if I would have encountered this image apart from the rest of the paintings in the show—even with the gas tanks—I would be hard pressed to find any discernible trace of a post-disaster environment. She could very well be looking to fill up her jet ski or motorcycle. In other words, the Venus is not reeling in post-hurricane Puerto Rico. She revels in it, for the Venus too is disastrous. There is no despair to contain. Rather, there's a pair of jean shorts and a too-short yellow crop top, which can barely contain her ample hips, buttocks, and breasts. As for dignity and valor, it's hard to say, but she certainly appears to be in no hurry to leave. María has her children to think about. The Venus just has her phone and her curlers and a pair of gas tanks. She has all the time in the world. She even had time to get her fingernails done.

Another painting features a decidedly white man in business attire, only his tie is a noose. He too is holding a gas tank. But contrary to the Venus, he appears to be on the brink of exhaustion, worn down from the waiting in line. While he does not possess María's dignified manner, his suffering is sobering. If one were to alternate glances between the Venus and him, one could easily envision them in line together. Well, not together. She would be in front, reveling in the moment, and he would be right behind, in quiet desperation, brought down by the aftermath of the disaster, but also by the disaster she embodies. The disaster of how her dress and her manner denote that the fabric of her life has not been radically made worse, that this is the social context where she can finally flourish. In this sense, the Venus is in the man's way. Or rather, she—not the long line, or the lack of electricity or the perishable food stuffs rotting at the docks or the botched hurricane relief effort from both the local and federal governments (Domonoske 2017)—is perceived as the true obstacle to his own flourishing. Thus, what he needs is for her to know better or to know her place, or to not take up the place of somebody like him, who, even as he would love to be able to get more gas for himself, is considerate of other people's needs.

The Venus, on the other hand, is anything but considerate. Because, really, who dares attempt to get more than their rightful share of essential supplies and goods? Who dares to not look the part of a bona fide member of a grief-stricken, precarious, post-disaster population? She should be ashamed of herself is what you imagine the flustered white man saying as the noose tightens around his neck. You imagine him saying it louder, so she hears him and turns, finally, to face him. But the Venus doesn't turn around because she's talking on her speaker phone. And so, because she never faces him, she never faces us either. She remains the aggregate of physical features and styling choices that we can identify (and judge) from behind and that, taken together, mark her as unruly in our collective imagination: curlers, jean shorts, red nail polish, tattoos, yellow crop top (Godreau 2018). Plus, she's Black. Or, if not Black, then certainly darker than him. Though, interestingly, her skin color is not the figure's main distinguishing feature. But it does become salient once one considers that the rest of the figures in the show—at least the dignified, suffering ones—are either grey, or blue, or white.

There's nothing in the promotional materials for the exhibition to suggest that the artist was interested in making a commentary about race in Puerto Rico. The paintings are simply about life on the island after the storm. A short review of the opening explains that the show, which the artist prepared with "a broken heart" seeks to capture "everything that the storm represented in his life" (Redacción 2018). And yet, there's the noose around the neck of the white man. And there's (white and) blue María and her children having to leave. And there's the (Black and) red Venus, in her place, just ahead of them, but going nowhere. It makes you wonder: how does race figure in the artist's heartbreak? Moreover, who or what is slowly killing the white man? Who or what is driving the white woman and her children out? What does the seeming comfort-in-place of the Black woman mean?

Also, why of all possible images would the artist choose a noose for the white Puerto Rican man?

White Privilege *en español*

During the 2020 election cycle, Alexandra Lúgaro, then the gubernatorial candidate for the upstart progressive party *Movimiento Victoria Ciudadana* (Citizen Victory Movement), did a Facebook Live on the topic of white privilege in Puerto Rico. Lúgaro, who identifies as white, discussed how skin color benefitted her and others in a myriad of social situations and scenarios on the island, and—offering a loose translation of Peggy McIntosh's famed piece on the subject—referred to white privilege as a sort of "invisible knapsack" that white residents carried, unbeknownst them, and which made their life better to the detriment of their dark-skinned or Afro Puerto Rican counterparts. This invisible knapsack, as envisioned by McIntosh (1989), contains "special provisions, maps, passports, codebooks, visas, clothes, tools and blank checks" that white subjects can access when needed within the course of their everyday life, without having to consciously claim these assets and tools, as they too are part of the social fabric of their everyday life.

Lúgaro's pronouncement on racism is noteworthy. It was, in fact, one of the few times a candidate for the governorship has broached the matter publicly, presenting it as an important factor of social life here. The livestream, of course, did not occur absent of a larger context. The sustained wave of on-the-street protest, media coverage, and larger public discussions on race and racism that spread across the world in the wake of the murder of George Floyd in Minneapolis extended to Puerto Rico, challenging the long-held— deeply engrained and institutionally enforced—view of Puerto Ricans as a "mixed" people who live in—and equally enjoy the benefits of—a sort of racial democracy. Lúgaro's statements on white privilege can thus be interpreted as a response to, and a part of, a larger effort to disrupt and destabilize the preeminent discourses on race on the island, which make invisible widespread patterns of both interpersonal and structural racism against Black people and Black culture (Godreau 2015). Her intervention becomes even more significant when one considers that rather than present racism as a problem for/of Afro Puerto Rican people, she instead opted to broach the matter as a problem of whiteness, that she as a white woman embodies.

Puerto Ricans, it must be said, have no problem identifying in terms of color. As it has been well documented, there exists a wide variety of colloquial terms that locals employ to refer to their own and others' skin color (Godreau 2015). However, it must also be noted, that, in general, there is a reticence to openly recognize the social consequences of race (Rebollo-Gil 2005). The problem, in part, has to do with the types of questions we ask. As Jorge Giovanetti (2016) astutely points out, racism on the island tends to be framed as a question of whether it exists, as opposed to the more adequate and potentially illuminating inquiry into how it manifests itself. This, to a certain degree can be explained. Racism here, as in other Latin American and Hispanic Caribbean contexts, in the words of my graduate school mentor, "is practiced as openly as it is passionately denied." This denial, unfortunately, often takes the form of, at least, five supposed social facts about race and racism in Puerto Rico that are repeated across a wide variety of social settings, including the academy. These are as follows:

1. Our national identity is based on the founding myth of *mestizaje* (race mixture), which, as a state-sponsored and enforced ideology, recognizes, and embraces, indigenous and African genealogies and cultural legacies, and thus acts as a type of built-in cultural buffer for widespread racism.
2. Racism in Puerto Rico did not assume the same legal, structural, or explicit forms it took on in the United States, where whiteness not only conformed the national identity but was also brutally enforced by way of Jim Crow segregation. As such, the race problem is of an interpersonal as opposed to systemic nature.
3. Regardless of whatever race effects may be noticeable in island society— class distinctions matter more than racial differences—seeing as *mestizaje*, as an ideology, has impeded the formation of both well-defined and potentially antagonistic, white and Black identities. Hence, the myriad of terms in the Puerto Rican vernacular that are widely used to identify oneself and others as neither properly white nor Black.

4) Racism in Puerto Rico, regardless of kind, manner, or extent, is decidedly less prevalent, or less harmful than in the United States.
5) Puerto Ricans, as colonial subjects, are not white.

While these social facts are not necessarily, and certainly not always, affirmed in tandem, and while they may appear in alternate, more nuanced forms, each has proven to be a mainstay in the more traditional literature on race and racism in Puerto Rico. According to this perspective, while instances of racial discrimination may occur, and while one can certainly trace strains of racist thought and imagery as well as certain social and cultural practices that denote racially exclusionary beliefs, racism need not be considered a significant social problem in Puerto Rico insomuch as race is simply not as important to islanders as other social markers. As such, while a considerable number of people may openly identify as white, the term is not immediately associated with interpersonal and/or institutional patterns of racial privilege and exclusion. Whiteness, nonetheless, has proven to be desirable in Puerto Rico. In the year 2000, 80.5 percent of respondents identified as white in the US Census. In 2010, 75.8 percent did the same. In 2020, and due to a dramatic rise in the "multiracial" category (with most respondents selecting "white and another race"), only 17.1 percent identified themselves as white (Cordero Mercado 2021). It is important to note that despite the deep drop in white-only identification, the category remained the preferred option in comparison to Black.

Now, while this prevailing sense of whiteness across the Puerto Rican population has been rightly linked to a deep-seated, widespread denial of blackness, there has not been a rigorous sustained consideration of what this turn to whiteness might signify in and of itself; specifically, how the desirability of whiteness across the island social space might imply that white racial identification affords discrete privileges to islanders. There is a gap, one could say, between recognizing the sway of whiteness among the Puerto Rican population and actively looking for its possible social effects. Two disparate, but ultimately related, events stand out.

In the featured plenary of the 2006 Puerto Rican Studies Association Conference held in Cornell University under the banner "Speaking the Unspoken: Race and its Intersections in the Puerto Rican Experience," historian

Luis Figueroa Martinez's opening remarks were as follows: "The problem of racism in Puerto Rico is the problem of white supremacy." From there he proceeded to argue that it was necessary for activists and academics to shift the focus of studies of race and racism from blackness to whiteness, and recognize that racism, as a project, is intent on potentiating a social context where white supremacy permeates all aspects of our collective life. The opposition was immediate and visceral. And it geared mainly around the allegedly ludicrous notion that there was such a thing as a Puerto Rican white subject. Figueroa Martinez was thus accused of carelessly attempting to impose the American racial construct of whiteness—understood here as a set of power relations that assign cultural, symbolic, and material capital to white individuals across generations (Feagin, Vera, and Batur 1994)—to a sociocultural context where white privilege finds no clearly identifiable manifestation outside of the most elite circles.

Fast forward to 2017 in Charlottesville, Virginia. When it came to light that one of the white supremacists arrested for acts of violence in a notorious white power rally was a Puerto Rican man, cultural critic and Afro Puerto Rican activist, Rosa Clemente explained this event as some sort of an outlier within the Puerto Rican cultural spectrum. She argued that the Puerto Rican white supremacist's "thinking is not uncommon *amongst a minority* of Puerto Ricans" (2017) [emphasis added]. Clemente's analyses, like the reaction to Figueroa Martinez's plenary address, are illustrative of the way most race scholars, activists, and cultural critics have attended to matters of whiteness and white privilege: as somehow strange, and/or confined to select groups. As a result, whiteness and white privilege have gone under-theorized even as there's been a boon of scholarship on Puerto Rican race relations over the past decade or so.

At present, the more critical and promising approaches to race and racism in Puerto Rico have shed light on the following:

1. How racial meanings and racist enforcement are tied to both class and place (Dinzey-Flores 2013).
2. How instances and patterns of state repression—especially those related to curtailing people's right to free speech—vary depending on protestors' race (LeBrón 2019).

3. How those quotidian, often fleeting and seemingly harmless instances of interpersonal racism, as well as those all-too-common instances of racist portrayals of blackness in the media (Rivero 2005), when taken as whole, signal an impressive, intricate network of racist aggression of varying kind and degree (Giovanetti 2016).

4. How, in even in the absence of explicit, systematic, state enforced forms of racial discrimination, access to housing, health services, education and employment vary markedly across racial lines (Lloréns, García-Quijano and Godreau 2017).

5. How images of blackness are strategically deployed in a manner that makes Black people at once integral to our national culture and inevitably foreign and dangerous (Godreau 2015; Rivera-Rideau 2015).

It is in this context where one could expect Puerto Rican whiteness studies to take root and flourish, complicating—and enriching—critical race scholarship on the island. Their relative scarcity explains, perhaps, why former candidate Lúgaro, in attempting to highlight the connection of whiteness and privilege on the island, turned to a US scholar and her landmark piece on white privilege "over there." Lúgaro, it should be noted, is not alone in this turn. One year prior, race scholar José Fusté took the myth of Puerto Rican racial democracy to task by calling out beloved local rapper—and international superstar—Residente for his white privilege. In a viral article, Fusté (2019)—responding to what were perceived to be racist comments made by the rapper against his African American counterparts—sought to teach Residente a valuable lesson on the workings of whiteness in Puerto Rico. To do so, Fusté also turned to McIntosh's white privilege exercise, applying it to what he presumed were the rapper's experiences growing up white, male, and lower middle class. In calling out Residente—an artist who for the past decade and half has sought to "represent" Puerto Rican identity—for his race privilege, Fusté, in a way, was calling out those cultural constructs that most of the population subscribes to, and that, as he correctly argues, are oriented toward whiteness, to the detriment of Afro-descendent peoples.

However, because the article is structured as a personal critique of Residente, the author substantiated his analysis of white privilege on select biographical details from the artist's upbringing: who his parents are, where he grew up, what type of schools he studied in. These details are taken at face value to convey an image of privilege that Fusté eagerly attributes to race: he studied in a private school, grew up in a gated community, his father is a well-known attorney and his mother a well-regarded actress. Driven, perhaps, by a desire to make his point as to the pervasiveness of white privilege in Puerto Rico, the author forgets to contextualize: due to the well-documented failures of the public education system, private schools abound, making "private," at best, a dubious marker of class status; neither theatre actors nor labor lawyers are necessarily well-paid professions; and an ever-increasing assortment of neighborhoods and communities from all across the social class spectrum are gated (Dinzey-Flores 2013). Thus, it is no wonder that Residente's highly autobiographical lyrics contain references to scarcity in the home, and on-the-street violence. And while these details do not necessarily negate the effects of race privilege in Residente's or any other white or light-skinned person's life in Puerto Rico, they certainly call for us—critics and scholars—to have greater care in properly situating and tracing out how white privilege manifests itself.

Consider, for example, Residente's 2020 hit song "René": a class-centered inventory of his life, the artist highlights his single mother making do, a childhood friend lost to police violence, once in a lifetime opportunity in the form of a scholarship. It is an inventory, a precarity common to many islanders' life, and that is not necessarily determined by race. Residente raps:

> Lower middle class, we were never owners/ the bank loan stole our dreams/ empty savings account/ but mom brightened our day dancing flamenco// she quit acting to take care of the four of us/ and we became her stage play/ she put our boots on/ and her life was made up of our triumphs and defeats. (my translation)

The elements the rapper highlights in this song in no way fit with the privileges the scholar assigns to him in the article. In fact, the disparity is so striking that one would be hard-pressed to even imagine the possibility of anybody, who has experienced what the artist has, envisioning themselves as the happy go lucky carriers of an invisible knapsack of privileges. This is Residente again: "I grew up together with Christopher, my friend/ we threw rocks together, broke a few windows/ ... //we were inseparable, until one day/ four cops killed him/ my happiness is still broken/ the lights went out in the ballpark" (my translation).

Still, the question remains as to how whiteness may bridge the gap between the precarity the rapper documents and the privilege the critic attributes to him. It should be noted that Residente's quick rise to fame in the early 2000s was commonly compared to that of white American rapper Eminem: though each, in his music, spoke of the financial hardships endured, both—it could be argued—benefitted in terms of media coverage and the like from being young white men immersed in a traditionally Black musical genre. Though both were scorned for the content of their lyrics—the family violence in Eminem, the political dissent in Residente—they instantly became poster boys for the genre, often leapfrogging more experienced or more proficient Black artists. In the case of Residente, part of the hoopla surrounding the artist allowed him to represent Puerto Rican people in a way that a Black rapper of the time like Tego Calderón—who like Residente made politically conscious, nationalistic (and Afrocentric) lyrics—could not. And so it is easy to identify how white privilege helps explain Residente's rise as an artist. And it would be logical to assume that there were also discrete privileges related to race at work during his upbringing. But these remain occluded by the specificities of the artist's life. Could one argue that Residente is alive today thanks to an invisible knapsack he carried on his back as he ran with his friend throwing rocks?

In recalling these two instances of recent antiracist public interventions—one a calling out of the self, and the other a denouncement of another—I want to call attention to the use of "white privilege," as both sociological concept and social phenomenon, in the Puerto Rican context. Both Lúgaro and Fusté turned toward McIntosh's analysis of whiteness in the United States to bring to light patterns of privilege and discrimination in Puerto Rico. While the use of McIntosh is readily explainable and justifiable, in that there has not been consistent talk of Puerto Rican racism as a problem of whiteness, thus leaving interested parties with little recourse but to pull from scholarly inventories developed elsewhere, I worry about the implications of such a quick and easy application of the concept to the Puerto Rican context.

Can white privilege operate as an invisible knapsack in a social and cultural context where identity and belonging are not, contrary to the United States, tied specifically to whiteness but rather to racial mixing? As Fusté himself notes, it's hard in the Puerto Rican context to tease specific race effects that though working in tandem with other structures of oppression—like class—are distinguishable from the rest. This, according to the author makes whiteness here harder to identify, oppose and ultimately dismantle. But I would argue also that because race—and therefore whiteness—is more fluid as an ideological structure of privilege and exclusion, it likely means that the set of privileges it offers are not as clear-cut, or life-defining as they are in the United States. They might be more precarious. Or fleeting.

I should note that most everything seems precarious in Puerto Rico today. The US colony is in the midst of a profound and prolonged economic depression made worse by the austerity politics imposed by local government. The local government, in turn, manages the public budget according to the strict guidelines set forth by a Federally appointed Fiscal Control Board. Because the Board's sole purpose is to identify and secure the necessary funds for repayment of the government's massive public debt, it has over the past five years required our elected officials to cut spending on essential services. Thus, while the island has become increasingly attractive for foreign investors, islanders have been migrating to the United States at a dizzying pace in hopes of attaining a better quality of life.

The question of how whiteness and white privilege figure into this scenario may very well be the "last thing" to consider in the face of rising social instability and individual and collective strife. But it *is* one thing that is missing from critical approaches to what life is like in Puerto Rico today. My proposition is that we cannot afford to leave out this one small thing if we are serious about figuring out what sort of life will be possible in Puerto Rico in the years to come.

3

A Small Book

My intention with this small book is to focus on some of the most notable, relevant and/or urgent manifestations of white privilege in Puerto Rico. I intend to do this, mostly, by sharing and critically reflecting on events, happenings that have taken place in (or around) my everyday life. In this regard, what follows will often seem diaristic. However, I should note that while "this [book] is consciously self-revelatory ... my purpose in writing it is sociological, not confessional" (Richardson 1997: 147). In turning a critical eye toward my own experience, I am looking to engage the social phenomenon of whiteness from a vulnerability that would offer readers a more engaging—and hopefully illuminating—text. My logic here is not that my life is somehow exemplary of whatever whiteness means in Puerto Rico, but that since I am very much a product of the social, discursive, and affective structures that produce and maintain white privilege on the island, the *I* that is me is as good a site as any for an inquiry. In this sense, you could say that this book is autoethnographic by default; especially as the bulk of it was written during the government-imposed lockdown during the Covid-19 pandemic. But, in all honesty, autoethnography strikes me as the ideal method for the study of a social phenomenon that seems to barely strike the surface of the recognizable in a society. Given the lack of open critical dialogue on matters of race and racism on the island, turning toward the self to study white privilege is not simply making do, it also makes sense: that which is difficult or uncomfortable or shameful to name—regarding experiences of privilege— is better undertaken as a task for oneself than imposed on another from the implicit comfort and distance of the researcher position. Furthermore, given the seeming "in-the-air" quality of whiteness and white privilege in purported racial democracies like Puerto Rico, a study of the self is more suited for the venture as it is not tasked with the production of results, but rather of "stylized interpretations" (Salvo 2020: 34): how I come to see white privilege as a significant element in my life/how it is not possible to adequately consider my life absent of a consideration of white privilege/in what ways is white privilege also inextricable from an adequate understanding of collective life in Puerto Rico. Tony Adams (2012: 186) explains, "With autoethnography, I can use my experience to call attention to the complexities of commonly held taken-for-granted assumptions, assumptions that might otherwise be difficult to critique."

I should note, however, that autoethnography as a method—and particularly as it pertains to self-studies of privilege—is not exempt from pitfalls in the analysis. That engaging one's privilege openly might bring forth feelings of shame and guilt does not mean that these ill feelings cannot become all too comfortable for the researcher. Autoethnographic analysis sometimes comes up short: an admission of privilege, and therefore a demonstration of vulnerability within critical writing can become the default landing point for critical studies of the self. It, suddenly and inexplicably, is *enough*—for purposes of critical thought—to admit to the social wrongness of one's life and have *that* be the contribution to the field. In this way autoethnographic research and writing can veer dangerously close to vanity projects. This book is not exempt from these dangers, and though I have sought to push myself and my thought processes beyond the comfort of self-serving admissions of guilt as it pertains to white privilege in Puerto Rico, it is possible that the analysis offered in these pages might, at times, come up short. For this, my apologies to you, dear reader.

These potential shortcomings notwithstanding, this small book does not limit its ethical–political vision. I am writing with the conviction that a critical race reading of both one's individual experience and of collective life in Puerto Rico is not only timely but necessary to the sort of thought that can and will contribute to de-colonial discourse and action within academic and activist circles in Puerto Rico. Autoethnographic writing, though focused on the singularity of one life is not constrained by the particularities of that life. Thus, whatever insight I can offer about whiteness and white privilege in my diaristic musings is ultimately social in nature. Similarly, whatever possibilities for radical change I identify in myself as white islander committed to antiracism are ultimately available to the rest of my white compatriots. In this sense, *Whiteness in Puerto Rico* though very much a book of me, is not properly about me.

My method of inquiry could best be described as idiosyncratic. In the chapters that follow I comment on current events, companion texts, personal recollections. I write, to be honest, about whatever helps to draw my attention to, and drive me into an inquiry of, whiteness in whatever way it manifests itself in present-day Puerto Rico. This, in part, is what makes the book so small. A commentated, whimsical, or willful (Ahmed 2014) personal inventory of white privilege in the colony. As such, it is shaped equally by my keen attention to certain events and issues, as well as by my wanton blindness to others.

What's more, in setting out to write it, I set for myself no clear path. I would simply sit with a hunch, idea, or with the admittedly modest daily goal to write something on or around the matter of whiteness. The best days were those when I had a story to tell, an anecdote that would allow me to demonstrate to you how white privilege operates here. Several of the chapters that make up the book are just that: anecdotes, stories. Many revolve around me. But, again, the book is not meant to read as a confession. As Laurel Richardson (1997: 58) notes, "Writing is an intentional activity and, as such, a site of moral responsibility." The *I* here is shorthand for *I am responsible*. My main responsibility to you is to make the writing a site of moral, ethical, and political engagement as well. Hence, the text is very much intended as a type of workbook for white antiracist academics and activists, in Puerto Rico and elsewhere. The end goal is to develop, revise, and continually rearticulate a daily practice of antiracism among those privileged by racist systems. I write about Puerto Rico because it is where I'm from and where I'm at. And because the fluid character of racial constructs and structures have made of whiteness and white privilege difficult topics to broach. A difficulty that often makes the issue a nonissue or allows for it to be attended to with less than ideal intellectual tools. Here's hoping I have chosen the right ones.

This is a small book with a rather long trajectory. To write about whiteness in Puerto Rico has been my "big" scholarly project since I entered graduate school almost twenty years ago. My dissertation touched on it. And over the years, I have attended to the matter in conference papers, poems, personal essays, and academic articles. But as I went on working through and around theoretical problems, and refining my arguments, the project became bigger and thus farther out of reach. The smallness of the book is my way of bridging the gap between the work I aspired to complete and what needs to be said about the matter—with conviction, concern, intellectual precision, self-awareness, and a definite sense of urgency—in the context and conditions of the proposed speaker.

The book is small in another important way: in places where race and racism have been historically understood as minor issues, always on the margins of public debate and discussion, regardless of the real-life effect they may have, to focus on whiteness can be perceived as paying attention to the least significant aspect of a less than important problem. After all, if one is to broach race and racism in purported racial democracies, one should be able to demonstrate how race and racism hinder people's quality of life. To explore race and racism should thus point to those dispossessed, those locked up, those killed by racial oppression. To study whiteness, and more specifically to study whiteness as experienced and understood by one individual, can readily and understandably be interpreted as a personal conceit presented under the guise of sociological inquiry proper. To this critique I would say that insofar as the system is designed to protect the privileged, to continue to engage the study of racism without directly broaching whiteness and white privilege is to cede too much ground in the road to understanding how racism as a system functions.

A small book like this will not, should not, take over much space within the discipline. I do hope however that it allows for, that it fosters, more ambitious, expansive and critical thought and discussion on the small matter of whiteness in Puerto Rico. Whiteness is only small to the degree that matters of skin color do not yet have an effective language for them to be broached in open, public dialogue. In other words, whiteness is only small because talk about race in Puerto Rico only occurs in spurts—usually at the heels of an incident that somehow manages to captivate the public's attention—and then dissipates again for indefinite periods of time, while the big social problems: economic crisis, gender violence, out migration, street crime and governmental corruption dominate both headlines, and public policy discussion. This is a small push to get considerations of race and racism into this area of concern.

One final note about the text, specifically about the type of theorizing to be done here. Perhaps "theorizing" is too big a word, a standard set too high. I am more inclined to consider the work an aggregate of musings regarding whiteness in Puerto Rico. This is not to imply that *Whiteness in Puerto Rico: Translation at a Loss* lacks scholarly rigor, or that the ideas collected here do not add up to a full set of principles that help explain how white privilege manifests itself on the island. It's just that theory, at least in my understanding, does not allow for how shaky so many "truths" regarding race in Puerto Rico appear to be. Readers will find that I will, at times, contradict myself in the following pages, as I rethink several of the more ambitious statements I make from chapter to chapter. The messiness of Puerto Rican racial structures, constructs, and discourses require, if not messy thinking, thought processes that embrace and work through the mess of race on the island. This, in turn, leads one to make contradictory claims as to the truth about race and racism here. Rather than attempt to eliminate or somehow reconcile these contradictions in my thought process on and around these matters, I have opted in turn to present them here as they arise.

Despite these contradictions, and perhaps because of them, there are a few clear propositions that can be gleaned from these pages.

A critical consideration of whiteness and white privilege is integral to any serious attempt to examine and understand racism in Puerto Rico today. To insist, as some still do, that race in Puerto Rico is *different* from race in the United States and therefore not a pressing social problem is to unwittingly declare one's investment in racial oppression. Furthermore, any study of racial ideology in the island can no longer insist on a fixed, clear line between American race thinking and Puerto Rican racial ideology. We can no longer presume that racial ideology in Puerto Rico is somehow the last remaining bastion of Puerto Rican identity that is unperturbed by American colonial influence. We must instead look at how one system corresponds to the other.

Because so much of Puerto Rican racist ideology is communicated in coded language, blackness—and whiteness—must be named openly. Thus, while it makes sense from a mobilization standpoint to insist on shared experiences of precarity for most of the island population, the possible effects of racial difference on these experiences must consistently be brought to the surface. It is possible that, given how deep and far-reaching precarity is on the island, to insist on privilege as something all white islanders have will do little to provoke people's critical engagement with race. Thus, it might prove more useful to focus on how questions of whiteness and blackness mediate and complicate experiences of precarity.

Having said this, white privilege is prevalent in Puerto Rico both within and beyond elite white circles. As such, the intellectual tools developed in the United States, for example, are useful in teasing this out. However, the sorts of privileges whiteness affords in Puerto Rico are specific to its social, political, and cultural context. Thus, concepts and tools from elsewhere should not simply be transported, translated, and applied. The fit of concepts and constructs is important. To insist on a social truth here simply because it is true over there is to further hinder efforts of critical race engagement and antiracism.

White islanders are crucial to any concerted effort of antiracism on the island. Whiteness too can be an awkward fit for bodies and selves. A pathway into antiracist thought and action might be to lean into that awkwardness. It is commonly believed that the best a white person can be in antiracist struggle is be an ally to a nonwhite people. This belief limits our individual and collective horizon of political action as it reduces our level of investment in antiracist thought and practice. As Tim Lensmire reminds us in his damning, yet hopefully pronouncement: "We white people are racist, down deep. But the deep down is neither monologic nor finished" (2017: 87).

Relatedly, this book looks to remind readers that liberatory gestures—quotidian, artistic, activist—are generous. One, at times, is too quick to dismiss antiracist interventions because of who the protagonists are, or on account of what we perceive to be its all too obvious faults, inconsistences, and so on. In doing so, we may very well miss out on what they *do* make visible or possible. Or what they may now have given us to further elaborate or build upon. May this small book, too, be something for others to build upon.

4

Dedication

This book is dedicated to the memory of Hernán Vera, my mentor in graduate school, who, in no small way, and still, a good fifteen years removed from our last long conversation on matters of race and racism, continues to impress upon me that there is no value to scholarly pursuits extricated from an agenda for liberation (Feagin and Vera 2008). Writing can be a method of sociological inquiry, yes. But only to the degree that it impresses upon both writer and readers our shared responsibility to be about what we write and read about.

Though I had heard of him, it took me a while to enroll in one of his classes. In my first seminar, we spent a good chunk of time listening to music. Classical, if I recall correctly. The lesson was supposed to be about race as ideology. It was all over my head, I admit. But I loved listening to him speak, pulling references across academic disciplines and traditions, as well as from literature, arts, popular culture, little known independent films and Hollywood blockbusters. I remember walking out of the classroom convinced that the study of race and racism required that one scavenge through all possible sources of knowledge at one's disposal. What I mean to say is not that one must become learned in a whole host of disciplines, but rather that race as a constitutive element of social life is present in all aspects of one's life and so one must seek to engage its study everywhere, at all times, no exceptions. This was the third time I had ever heard him speak.

The second was at a forum I helped organize for the Puerto Rican Students Association. I invited him at the behest of my English professor Jim Haskins, who conditioned his own participation on Hernán's presence. The forum was about images of whiteness and blackness in the Latinx community. My other invitees were white or white-passing Latinx professors, who Haskins did not personally know. He told me that if I had the gall to feature him as the token

Black face on a racism panel, then he should at least have one white person there he could trust. I can't remember if I picked up on his calling me out, but I patiently waited outside of Hernán's office, introduced myself and extended a warm invitation. He asked if "Jim" sent me. I nodded. Then he lectured me on how antiracism is about the risk one person undertakes in making a call and the responsibility of another to answer it. Though I listened closely, I had no idea what he meant. But was relieved when he accepted.

I ended up having to make two different sets of flyers for the event. Haskins, upon seeing the first batch up on campus, scolded me for not including any of the presenters' names: "If you call on others for help, you better call us by our names."

In the forum, Hernán dissected a set of media images from both Chile and the United States to speak about white racism as an intergenerational, transcultural, and transnational project. He seemed intent to impress upon the audience that there was no such thing as safe quarter from the abuses and trappings of whiteness. Trappings like selecting an overwhelmingly white or white-passing panel for a discussion on race and racism. Abuses like not naming the people who are to speak on the matter at your behest.

Haskins, it should be noted, had a reputation for making white students cry in the classroom. I was never sure as to how he saw me. With regards to race, I mean. I remember I spoke in class from the perspective of a student of color. And since he never challenged me on it, I assumed that's how he saw me. Plus, only the white kids left the room crying and I never felt the urge or need. It was a performance, of course. I had this idea—accurate or not—that the racial class markers from my place of birth did not translate well in the American South, which allowed me to "rest" from my critical accounting of them, at least in public. There's no way Haskins did not see through me. He just opted to press me in more subtle ways. I remember, for example, presenting on Toni Morrison's *Playing in the Dark* in class. As part of my presentation, I read the following passage aloud:

> Writing and reading are not all that distinct for a writer. Both exercises require being alert and ready for unaccountable beauty, for the intricacies or simple elegance of the writer's imagination, for the world that imagination evokes. Both require being mindful of the places where imagination sabotages itself, locks its own gates, pollutes its vision. Writing and reading mean being

aware of the writer's notions of risk and safety, the serene achievement of, or sweaty fight for, meaning and response-ability. (1992: xi)

Then I opted for what was my go-to strategy when engaging serious discussions of race. I proposed a comparison between the American landscape as imagined by white American authors and the Puerto Rican imagination. I remember he interrupted me to ask, "The Puerto Rican imagination? Aren't you missing a qualifier mister Rebollo? Is that the best you can do after reading Ms. Morrison's text? Might not your imagination be sabotaging itself right now, polluting your vision?" I remember understanding exactly what he meant but was unwilling to break my comfortable performance of a nonwhite student. And so, I did not add the qualifier: "white" Puerto Rican, whose unchecked investment in whiteness, sabotages his imagination. A week or so after my presentation, I approached Haskins with the idea for the panel. Hernán, I understood then, was the condition I had to meet to secure my professor's participation. Hernán, I understand now, was Haskins's tender way of helping repair my imagination.

Here is where Hernán was brilliant in attending to racial constructs across different national and cultural contexts: he always prioritized correspondences between social systems, cultural traditions and practices, behavioral patterns, and social phenomena. Whereas students would be eager to look for, identify, and "unpack" whatever seemed to be unique about racial ideology in other societies, Hernán insisted we consider the question of how the object of study might serve whiteness. For Hernán, what made something unique—at least as it pertained to the study of race and racism—was its potential for liberation. Thus, he insisted, if we were able to identify a service to whiteness—no matter how remote—then the object was not unique; it simply corresponded to phenomena and formations we weren't accustomed to.

Thanks to Hernán and Haskins, I learned that most everything in society is at the service of whiteness. What we, as scholars, must do is effectively highlight and explain how everything around us performs such a nefarious service. A way out of whiteness will appear, Hernán used to say, once most everything around us has been illuminated.

This book is a modest contribution to the struggle for illumination. It is dedicated to my two professors. This dedication, I want to say, following Jane

Gallop (2002: 5), "is integral, intrinsic to the theorizing" insomuch as the book collects some of my best attempts at repairing my imagination. And, perhaps, it would not have occurred to me that such repair was even necessary if it weren't for Haskins. And, perhaps, I would have never found the necessary tools and resources to undertake such work if it hadn't been for Hernán. This is Gallop again, "I want the dedication to my [professors] to be more than an extrinsic gesture; I want the dedication to be inseparable from the main point of the [book]" (137). The point is this:

Dr. James Haskins

Dr. Hernán Vera

If by chance you called, this is my answer.

5

A Problem

I am what you—if you were from and in Puerto Rico—would call a *blanquito*. A literal English translation would be "little white," but this translation would prove useless. A more accurate alternative would be "privileged white." But this translation also fails to communicate the genius of the original Spanish. *Blanquito* condenses extreme racial and class privilege in Puerto Rico into a single, seemingly innocuous and, to the unexperienced, tender term. It's the diminutive, that does it, which would appear to signal endearment as opposed to condescension. In truth, it communicates a level of derision that one would be hard-pressed to find in any other word in the Puerto Rican vernacular, without getting downright gross and vulgar. And that precisely is the other key aspect of its genius: *blanquito*, as an insult, is a safe word. It's offensive without being crude. You can say it pretty much anywhere, without fear of hurting anyone's feelings except the person you're referring to.

More importantly, *blanquito* foregrounds race. A frequently used synonym, *guaynabito* (or its cruder version *guaynabicho*), which is used to refer to white and wealthy people from the municipality of Guaynabo, foregrounds place and class. The latter term is more recent, and one could very well argue that its more widespread use over the past decade or so is a straight byproduct of the municipality's growth and development under a notorious former mayor, who transformed it into a haven for upwardly mobile suburban families. Still, the truth is that the term is less contentious for the Puerto Rican imaginary. *Guaynabito* implies that privilege is solely material. Moreover, it implies that it is confined to a particular geography. As such, it is contained in a relatively small social and physical bubble that, due to residents' extreme social isolation, really has no bearing on island life. *Blanquito*, on the contrary, implies a more insidious form of privilege, tied to skin color, but not to a particular place. It is embodied. It moves. It points to something deeper, and more ample, than residential address. More importantly, it means that there is something to whiteness. That whiteness somehow plays into the question of who gets to live where, and how. That whiteness is somehow relevant to people's quality of life. And that while only a select few could ever afford to live in Guaynabo's signature suburbs, census data would suggest that whiteness is desired and, apparently, accessible.

The problem is that the term *blanquito*—even within critical writing—is as dismissive of the figure as it is derisive. For literary scholar Juan Duchesne (2008), for example, *blanquitos* are zombies, caught in a cycle of consumption. Drained of individuality, they are interested in whatever their class status and bank account demand that they be interested in: golf, vacations, luxury goods. As such, they are only threatening to the extent that they serve as a stark reminder to how both national and individual self-worth can be surrendered by buying into the allure of American neoliberalism. Race, it should be noted, does not figure anywhere in this analysis. *Blanquitos* are defined by their place of residence, the exclusivity of their social circles, their emptiness, and an apparent inability to communicate. For Duchesne, the principle marking of this group is its members' speech patterns: a sort of Spanglish, that speaks not to the history of dispossession, migration to the United States, and the steady flow of cultural remittances between the mainland and the island, but to an exposure to (and predilection for) American culture that is more a product of staying in and watching television than of being in any way exposed to the complexities of life in an American colony.

Famed novelist and cultural critic Edgardo Rodríguez Juliá, in his short essay "Blue Experts" (2011), shares Duchesne's view as it pertains to the zombie-like quality of this younger generation, but contrary to him, Rodríguez Juliá does not disregard them. According to him, these are either the kids of present heads of state and the political leaders of the future. So, while they—in their present form—might seem laughable, their values, world vision will end up shaping Puerto Rican society and culture. Also, Rodríguez Juliá, at least, notes that "almost all of them are white." The comment reads like an aside. Like an observation that barely made it into the final version of his essay. As if it were a small thing. The implication here, of course, is that while most *blanquitos* are white, not all of them are. Or must be. In this sense, *blanquito* is more a question of attitude than of phenotype and socioeconomic background.

While I am not a proponent of this view, as it serves to de-emphasize the strong racial content of the term, one could argue that the focus on *blanquito* as more a marker of an attitude than of skin color does have an upside. If even Black or dark-skinned Puerto Ricans can be *blanquitos*, so long as they have the class status to back it up, it implies that white privilege takes on distinct, readily identifiable forms—mode of dress and address, tastes—that extend beyond white bodies. To say then that it is more a matter of attitude than of race does not necessarily mean that race matters less in the island but that so many aspects of social life and personhood are experienced and interpreted as raced effects. The social context—contrary to, for example, the United States—allows for you to pass for white, so long as you act white. Now this has often been interpreted as indicative of greater social mobility, of a more fluid racial hierarchy. This is incorrect. Fluidity would seem to imply that people can—by, for example, reaching a higher income bracket—be freed of the discriminatory and harmful constrictions of blackness. That the question of race or skin color retreats to the background because, as they say, "money whitens." Jossianna Arroyo (2014), however, reminds us that in Puerto Rico where you're from never ceases to matter, as evidenced by the common expression *yo sé donde tú saliste* (I know where you came out of), leveled as a threat to people who have bettered their lot in life. Or more precisely who were not born into the race-class group they now find themselves in. And because where you're from is so imbricated with who or what you are, the underlying logic of this threat is that a change in social conditions does not imply a change in one's social standing proper. In this sense, there is no such thing as becoming a *blanquito*, whether by a change in attitude or an increase in income or wealth. You are either born into it or you're not.

To date, the best definition of *blanquitos* was offered by journalist Dennise Y. Pérez (2014) in a short op ed piece about, paradoxically, *guaynabitos*. Pérez writes:

> Guaynabito: an upper middle class and upper class person that lives in a gated community within the territorial limits of Guaynabo City, who does their shopping at the outlets, in San Juan, or in Miami and New York, but never in (the neighboring municipality of) Bayamón, and who has children

enrolled in bilingual schools and pokes fun at the UPR (IUPI for those of us who are not guaynabitos) when their son starts applying to universities. My apologies, when he starts looking at colleges. In summary, a blanquito. (my translation)

While Pérez insists on the term as an almost exclusive marker of class, character, and attitude, her articulation—regardless of intent—manages to catch the often evasive, and messy, essence of white privilege, race, and racism in Puerto Rico. It's the final line that does it: in summary, a *blanquito*. Race seemingly comes out of nowhere at the end. Nothing in the earlier description even hints at skin color as being an integral part of the construct. It's included at the very end, first, to indicate that race has something—which remains unidentified and unexplained—to do with wealth and social privilege on the island. But, most importantly, for Pérez, it's the race-specific term—the term that foregrounds whiteness, which she is relying on for the concept of *guaynabito* to be understood by her readers. The underlying logic of her definition is that race—and whiteness, particularly—undergirds recognizable forms of social privilege and exclusion, which are not explicitly talked about as race-related but are ultimately understood as raced effects: where you live, where you study, how you speak, who and what you are expected to be across the course of your life.

I am, in summary, a *blanquito*, which is to say that the knowledge I have of island life—at least the one I accrued during my formative years—amounts to an intimate inventory of prejudices that reduce the people and places outside of my race–class group to objects of my (forbidden) fancy or fear. Suffice to say that I very much spoke the sort of Spanglish that Duchesne ridiculed and that I most certainly learned from countless hours spent in front of the TV. Suffice to say that I grew up knowing very little if anything about the history of the island of my birth but was constantly reminded of how I was part of the best the island of my birth had to offer. Suffice to say that if I were to draft an affective geography of my life, the key spaces, and places, where my life took place all comfortably fit within Pérez's description of who and what *blanquitos* are. What we are, ultimately, is a threat to any remaining hope and potential of a dignified life for the vast majority of the island population. As arbitrary budget cuts and privatization of essential services continue to define public policy in Puerto Rico, only *blanquitos* will thrive here, as only *blanquitos* can afford to live without the most obvious and urgent publicly funded programs, including but not limited to housing, education, transportation, healthcare, and employment. This is how austerity serves whiteness. It creates the conditions where only people like me can afford to make a life for themselves and their children here. This is why *blanquitos* as a group deserve the derision they are often subjected to, but this is also why they should not be so easily dismissed as local critics are often prone to do.

I am, what you could call, a problem.

6

How *Blanquitos* Belong

In 2004, as part of my dissertation research (Rebollo-Gil 2005), I had the opportunity to sit with and interview a handful of young men and women, who identified themselves—however begrudgingly—as *blanquitos*. Two interviewees stood out. They were both 22-year-old males. They had studied in elite private schools on the island, attended US colleges, and were, at the time, back home, looking to embark on their professional careers. Fernando had just entered law school and was interning with a lawyer friend of his family. Benny was working as a bank loan officer while he figured out his next move. What made my conversations with them notable, among other respondents at similar life stages and from similar socioeconomic positions, was the striking openness with which they spoke about how they perceived themselves within the Puerto Rican racial and social spectrum. Whereas most interviewees manifested discomfort, difficulty, and even unwillingness to speak about their experience in raced terms, Fernando and Benny seemed to welcome the opportunity to speak on these matters. This willingness to speak corresponded with the relative ease with which they recognized and accepted their position as young privileged white men, even if such recognition brought considerable existential grief to each of them. Because I have not encountered such candid self-awareness from a *blanquito* identity in other scholarly, artistic and/or media productions, I wanted to revisit these interviews here.

After commenting on his upbringing as a member of an elite family, I asked Fernando if he ever felt estranged from fellow Puerto Ricans, outside of those exclusive circles:

> Sometimes they talk to you in English, man. Like I go up to pay in a store and they answer me in English … and if I'm in the resort, forget it. You know, they're never going to talk in English to a person who's more typical or

average looking. [Q. How does that make you feel?] Well, it's not that if affects me a lot but at that moment you don't feel very well. You feel alienated, like a foreigner in your own country. They don't see that you're Puerto Rican and that's a way to alienate you from what you really are. (Rebollo-Gil 2005: 82)

While at the time of the interview—and of the subsequent analysis—I was mostly interested in how certain physical markers—Fernando has pale white skin, light-colored eyes, and brownish-blond hair—were read as American by others, I am struck now by the specific site of the encounters he opted to recount. In Fernando's mind, "average" or "typical" Puerto Ricans are to be found working in retail stores, part of the staff at his favorite resort. They are not his neighbors, nor his classmates, nor his work colleagues. They are not part of his faith community, nor are they even the people that might sit next to him on a bus (Fernando drives a luxury car), on a plane (he always flies first class), or even at a concert (he gets box seats). Thus, a sense of belonging would not be possible even if they spoke to him in Spanish. As such, whereas, in Fernando's mind, "what you really are" is Puerto Rican too, what he really is is disconnected, separate, alien to whatever Puerto Ricans, in socioeconomic terms, are as a group. In this sense, Fernando chooses to gripe about the question of language only because it makes the gap between himself and whoever is serving him seem like an unjust affront on their part; as if they were misreading, and taking something from, him. The identification of, and fixation with, language as the problem enables Fernando to avoid openly acknowledging the truly significant differences between himself and most island peoples: while they might coincide in the resort as guest and hotel staff, they do not inhabit the same island space.

While I doubt about the sincerity of his pain, this focus on alienation strikes me as significant. For Fernando there is an existential cost to being who he is, belonging to the race and class group he belongs to. Getting his feelings hurt by an English-language greeting seems to imply a failure to connect with—make a valid claim to—an "authentic" Puerto Rican identity, which only those who serve him could bestow upon him. Puerto Rico then, when considered in relation to the rest of his compatriots, remains inaccessible as home. He only truly feels like he belongs here when he considers local social mores in relation to those his white Americans must abide by. Consider the following response to the question of, given his experience stateside, what the main difference was between race relations in the United States and on the island. According to Fernando,

> Also, in the US you say the word "negro" in English—"N*****"—and you create this chaos. However, in Puerto Rico in high school if there was one or two of the kids who was *really really* Black, you would just call him "el negro" and that was it. Problem solved. It simply wasn't an issue like in the States. (Rebollo-Gil 2005: 98; emphasis added)

This is what being Puerto Rican *does* for him: it affords him the cultural grammar to publicly acknowledge racial difference, to mark and assign others a racially inferior position without it becoming an issue. For Fernando, then, the fluidity of the island racial spectrum allows him, as a *blanquito*, the opportunity to live whiteness more freely. In reading one quote against the other, Puerto Rico emerges as a problem for the privileged white subject, as his features (and his social location) render him foreign, and on the other, Puerto Rico emerges as the haven of the privileged white subject, as racism can be openly expressed with impunity: you would just call him *el negro* (the Black guy) and that was it.

I should note the mis-translation at the center of this quote from Fernando. *Negro* is Spanish for black. There is no Spanish equivalent for the racist epithet "n*****." That Fernando, when reflecting on how to publicly refer to his Black counterparts in both Puerto Rico and the United States, chooses to give that nefarious meaning to the otherwise un-derogatory Spanish term, points to an increased awareness of racial difference and inequality in Puerto Rico, and, importantly, signals a high level of racist action on the part of Fernando: when he refers to somebody as a Black in Puerto Rico, he is in effect calling them a "n*****" in public, without fear of reprimand.

This freedom to exercise privilege is premised on a perceived willingness of Afro Puerto Ricans to know their place vis-à-vis their white compatriots, or an apparent inability to manifest their opposition. This, I think, is what that absence of "chaos" means: the mere utterance of the racist epithet "over there" would bring about complaint. In Puerto Rico, there is silence. Whiteness has no discernible public opposition.

This, however, does not mean that privileged whites are fully comfortable here. Because Puerto Rican culture does not explicitly distinguish nor determine belonging based on race, the distance privileged whites can put between themselves and the rest of the island population finds a hard ideological limit: we are all one people. As such, *blanquitos* cannot help but see themselves, if not reflected in "those people," somehow caught up with them. And while, in Fernando's case, he seems to long for recognition, there exists also a deep concern among the privileged that they cannot shake off their less than fortunate compatriots. The messiness of local racial constructs implies that there are no clear-cut distinctions to be made between groups. *Blanquitos* must make sure to police and protect the spaces, manners, and idioms most dear to them. This is Benny, the bank loan official, explaining his frustrations with what he felt was the "average" Puerto Rican:

> Listen, I was super patriotic. I was like super stereotypical with my beliefs in independence for Puerto Rico, my Che Guevara T-shirts, and my protests. It's just that now there is no turning back. We're in a hole and what we need are like two cruise ships and we get all the *cafres* [low class, thugs] in and we put a bomb in each one and we'll kill all the *cafres* that way. Because they don't want to educate themselves and admit that they're in the wrong and I'm not going to be able to change them. (Rebollo-Gil 2005: 130–1)

Here, Fernando's ease corresponds to Benny's burden: the latter has been made to witness the ruin that his countrymen and women have been made into, on account of not having the adequate cultural tools to Americanize properly. And so, while Fernando balks at being greeted by a store worker in English, Benny balks at the image of that very same store worker—or somebody like them, or close to them—acting out. Of course, Benny doesn't ever get to see them. At least not up close. At least not somewhere other than the airport or maybe the mall or perhaps in line at a gas station in the aftermath of a major hurricane. But it's enough for him to know that they are out there and that their existence is inextricably tied to his. So, while neither young man might feel like they properly belong to Puerto Rico, Benny certainly manifests a sense of being bound to the people here, and thus of feeling brought down by them. And this feeling, at least for him, threatens to become intolerable, to the point of devising and sharing a violent fantasy of a sort of social purge.

I would like to offer these two initial coordinates for a map-in-the-making of *blanquito* subjectivities in Puerto Rico: alienation and cruelty. *Blanquitos* feel cast out by the people they are supposed to be a part of due to their perceived lack of authenticity. But they are also put off by these same people and the apparent inevitability of their connection to them. They are caught between a desire to be accepted by and a desire to eradicate their less-than-privileged counterparts. This, I propose, is the noose around the white man's neck in Rinaldi's painting. Puerto Rico is the place where *blanquitos* most perfectly fit, in the sense of being able to fully act out on their racial and class privilege, but Puerto Rico is also very much ill-fitting as they do not fully see themselves—their taste, mode of life, and so on—readily reflected in everyday life on the island. This makes life here almost unbearable for them, and yet their life *is* here. In any other place, even if their race and class privilege would translate well, they would lose the sociocultural context that maximizes said privileges by imbuing them with personal and collective meaning that transcends material wealth. Both Benny and Fernando were proud to carry their respective family name, to live up their family's expectations of them, and to ultimately see themselves as the rightful bearers of their family's high social standing. This, at the end, was the type of authenticity that truly mattered to them. It just so happens that it was adhered to this place and so they were forced to constantly negotiate the terms of their national and cultural belonging too. To be a *blanquito*, in this regard, is both a gift and a curse: a noose that sits loose around their necks.

I remember being put off by these two interviews. I remember being openly more critical, as an interviewer, of their responses, struggling to hide my distaste. But I also remember recognizing their angst as my own. Looking back on my childhood and adolescence, it's hard for me to recall a physical or social space that I frequented where I was not immediately identifiable and treated as my father's son, where to be treated as my father's son did not imply receiving special treatment. In this context of privilege, nothing is earned, of course. The burden, if any, is that of having to prove yourself as worthy of all that has been given and will continue to be given to you. One does not know it at the time, but what is given—what I was given—is this discrete sense of having been chosen for a life that is embarrassingly better than that of the people you are supposed to belong to but will hardly ever see, much less come into meaningful contact with, outside of having to depend on their services for the purposes of living your life to the fullest. And yet, one does come to know rather early. I came to know early the nature of this terrible gift, of which I had to prove myself worthy. The gift shows itself in the faces of the people who are there to be of service to you. It shows itself in the faces of the people you cannot bear to look at or cannot stand, but of whom you ask the one thing they can keep from you: acknowledgment. An acknowledgment that cleanses the social violence inherent in your interactions with them. This is what is at the root of Fernando's complaint of resort staff. It is also at the root of Benny's fantasies of death and destruction. A feeling lingers in the mind and heart of the *blanquito* that the privilege that has formed and informed his life as a natural occurring phenomenon is not in fact natural nor accepted. That to prove himself as worthy of this privilege to his family, he needs to show that he can live with that lingering feeling that his entire life is a forceful taking from another. And that the other knows it. And recognizes him for what he is.

7

Scandal

The Pandemic Unemployment Assistance (PUA) scheme, allegedly concocted by a parent of a student in the island's elite Jesuit school, resulted in some thirty kids, between the ages of fourteen and eighteen, applying for and receiving up to $8,000—a special compensation paid by the US Federal Government to individuals who became unemployed on account of the Covid-19 pandemic. The parent provided them with the name of a fake place of business, from which the students reported being laid off. The money was used for cars, Airbnb retreats, electronics, and luxury items. As the story developed, rumors began swirling online about the possibility of students from other private schools taking part in the same or in similar schemes. No names were officially released, though a subpoena was served at the Jesuit school for the administration to grant access to student records. It is unclear if access was ever granted. Seven months after the initial story broke and following sporadic reports of several unidentified families repaying the money, the case was officially closed, without a single arrest (Díaz Rolón 2021). Moreover, contrary to how the story was first reported and how a police spokesperson had confirmed at the time, the Secretary of Justice stated that there were never multiple cases related to one school, but a single isolated case of a minor who happened to be a student in the Jesuit school.

I want to say that the handling of this incident by the justice department most clearly illustrates how white privilege transcends the apparent social and physical bubbles the *blanquitos* inhabit: whiteness and its corresponding privileges are takings. While tens of thousands of islanders were waiting for their PUA applications to be attended to—a painstaking process riddled with mismanagement and misinformation issues—a group of teenage boys from social circles where the concept of governmental assistance registers, at best, as alien, colluded to take up time and funds from those with both rightful claims and urgent needs.

I graduated from the Jesuit school. As did my uncles, brothers and most of my cousins. None of us have been found guilty of fraud, and I would venture to say that most—if not all—of my family members would likely frown at the students' alleged actions. They likely would not point to the school as responsible, and—barring personal animosities—would not point to the students' families, as they likely know them or know of them: perhaps the students' fathers or uncles, their older brothers or cousins were classmates of ours. Explanations must be found elsewhere. Considering the number of students initially reported to have been involved and the age variance, it would be hard to dismiss the event as the unfortunate, and ultimately bizarre, undertaking of a few "bad apples." An acquaintance—mother to a pair of graduates—for example, speculated about the possible involvement of teachers or other school staff, who, unbeknownst to both the students and their parents, may have gotten hold of the kids' personal information and submitted the fraudulent applications on their behalf. Or, maybe, the kids were involved, having been recruited by a trusted, but ultimately malicious, teacher or staff member. This type of speculation is outwardly premised on a refusal to believe that the younger generations—the future of this country—is already corrupt. But I would venture to say that the unwillingness to even consider collusion between students and parents, which in turn drives the need to actively—and perhaps even desperately—look for alternative explanations, however implausible, is indicative of a deeper, stronger refusal to point to and find whiteness at fault.

Seeing these kids in all their complexity, refusing to jump to judgment and pausing to not only consider context but also to push themselves to propose alternative explanations, no matter how implausible these might be, is seeing (and serving) whiteness. Especially, when those alternative explanations center on the imagined ill-intent of those outside their exclusive social circles. It's not that teachers and staff are known, or even imagined, to be Black. What is known is that they—based on their modest salaries—are presumed to live in close proximity to more marginal, and thus, likely Black, or at least not *blanquito*-white, segments of the island population. My acquaintance, to defend her position, asked, "What possible need could *our* school kids have [to do this]?" (emphasis added).

The question, though rhetorical, merits a response. But first, a brief exploration into need is in order. What the students don't need, from the woman's perspective, is the money. Nor, ultimately, the things reportedly purchased with the money. As these are types of things—staycations, luxury vehicles, electronics—that they already have or will have eventually. Lack of material need implies that their alleged bad acts can only be attributed to their bad character. And she cannot fathom this possibility. Enter the malevolent teacher or staff person, who is presumably both needy and criminally inclined. They are needy as private school salaries in Puerto Rico are notoriously unjust, but this identifiable material need is already [and always will be] superseded by their bad character, as according to my acquaintance's conspiracy theory, they recruited otherwise noble and un-needy students to do their bidding. And so, the question "what need could they possibly have?" is not actually a question but a statement of ideology: they are innocent. And a witch hunt: there must be somebody else, somebody below them, that can be made responsible.

The woman's rationale here is a constitutive element of whiteness as a social force. While, judging from the press, this investigation was totally and exclusively directed at the students and their respective parents, there is always a protective layer that must be pierced for privileged whites to become the object of scrutiny and be held to account for their alleged bad acts. Typically, as in the Jesuit school case, this protection is attributed principally, if not exclusively, to class standing or status, but I would argue, it responds to race as well.

Consider, for example, the case of Pablo Casellas. The adult son of a federal judge, Casellas was convicted of murdering his wife in the pool area of their residence in an exclusive Guaynabo City gated community. Upon being initially questioned by officers, Casellas alleged that a *negrito* (Black man) had jumped the fence and killed his wife. Though, from the start and in consideration to the available evidence, the story seemed implausible, and though the state police formally dismissed this theory of the crime, officers rounded up young Black males from the neighboring working-class community of Los Filtros and took them in for questioning. Nothing came of it. And public attention shifted to the minutia of his arrest, trial, and conviction. Still, young Black men or Black-looking men were taken in for questioning on the flimsiest of causes for suspicion. The police, then, acted on my acquaintance's rationale: Casellas is innocent. There must be somebody else, somebody below him, that can be made responsible. That somebody is Black, or close to Black with regards to place, class, and social status.

Now, one could easily consider the event as described above and explain it solely as a function of Casellas' privilege, which, even within the most precarious of situations as a suspect to his wife's murder, allowed him to sway the police and divert time and resources to the harassment of poor Black males. To a certain extent, you could say that it doesn't matter that Casellas was white, what matters is that he was the son of a federal judge and a Guaynabo city resident. Yet, according to reports, Casellas did not state where the supposed Black assailant was from. The decision to look for him in Los Filtros—to look for him outside of the gated community—was made by officers. The impossible tale told by the then murder suspect was not only acted upon but also aided by another impossibility, of a different sort—Casellas cannot have any Black neighbors. The first impossibility is ideological (the white son of a federal judge cannot be guilty of such a crime). The second is a social fact (the Puerto Rican landscape is segregated by race). The combination of the two resulted in a veritable witch hunt, with discrete consequences: a student of mine at the time was among the people arrested. The witch hunt, in turn, ensures that the presumed all-white neighbors are protected.

Legal scholar Katheryn Russell Brown, in studying similar claims of wrongdoing made by white American individuals against Black Americans, refers to these instances as racial hoaxes. She explains (1996: 595), "A racial hoax occurs when (1) someone fabricates a crime then blames it on, for example, a Black person; or (2) an actual crime has been committed and someone falsely blames, for example, a Black person." The key here is that this sort of hoax is only effective in societies where anti-Black racism is widespread. What made Casellas's claim even remotely believable—even before considering who his father was—is the social construct of blackness, and Black men especially, as inherently dangerous, or criminal. In other words, *negrito*, as used in this context—and to be frank, by any rightful resident of the gated community—was already and always going to be understood as code for intruder. As such, the information given to authorities by Casellas not only had to be given serious consideration, but it also had to be acted on, thus shielding—however temporarily—both the principal suspect and the elite community he belongs to from further police intervention and scrutiny.

Since news of the Jesuit school PUA scandal broke, the police have made at least twelve arrests for fraudulent claims. Most of the reported arrests have taken place in banks, as the guilty attempted to cash their checks. Among those arrested was a 47-year-old homeless man, apprehended with four separate checks totaling up to upwards of $50,000 in federal funds. Another arrestee was a seventeen-year-old high school student, apprehended in a bank terminal while cashing a check for $8,058. He was a student at San Juan area public school. It is unclear what either of them needed the money for.

One would have to question the supreme diligence of the state—in close communication and collaboration with private banks—in rounding up individual schemers from presumably all walks of life in the face of the state's apparent disinterest in prosecuting what was reported to be a complex, coordinated effort to commit fraud. For the cynical, the difference is due exclusively to a question of power, and privilege and influence. The cynics are certainly right. But one would have to say that the arrest of the public-school student crystallizes what power and privilege, and influence, are in the service of: a white future. The whiteness, in this case, of the school as a social space, as it is spared the media spectacle of police arriving on the grounds with a subpoena for student records. The whiteness, too, of the homes and neighborhoods where the students and their families live, as they were also spared the spectacle of home arrests. The whiteness, it should be said, of the parents of the kids involved, as well as that of other families, like mine, who belong to school's intergenerational community, live in those same neighborhoods and either know each other, or know of each other, who thanks to the inaction of the government in working the case, get to move on, while the families of other kids who acted in a similarly criminal manner—but with actual need, perhaps—face embarrassment, fear, wrecked reputations, and possible prosecution.

It's hard to speculate what may come of the case against the student. But just the simple fact that he was arrested on site, that while even when his parents are not reported to have any involvement in the actions he allegedly carried out, they still were not able to secure his future to the same extent and with the same efficiency that even the guilty parents of some of the Jesuit school kids were able to do for their children, speaks to the type of futures that are possible in Puerto Rico. This future is not solely about what these kids avoided: arrest, criminal charges, sullied reputations, decreased college, and job prospects. It is that the school, the community, family, the race–class group they belong to will likely absorb their bad acts, thus not simply absolving them of responsibility, but buttressing this absolution on the social and moral good that *that* school, *that* community, *that* family, and *that* race–class group represent. The public-school kid could even be let go with a stern warning and he would still have to deal with the consequences of his actions, even if those consequences did not surpass the realm of personal fear and public shame. He is, for all intents and purposes, alone in the world. The Jesuit school kids—at bare minimum— have the rich tradition of the school who—everybody knows—produces the brightest, most promising young men, some of the best the country has to offer. Whereas public schools, everybody knows, are just teeming with "bad apples." That is why responsible parents, however powerless they may be, do all that is in their power to enroll their kids in private institutions.

The Jesuit school by the way is heralded for its generous scholarship program.

8

Scandal, Too

In July 2019, then governor Ricardo Rosselló was forced to resign amid a wave of massive on-the-street protest and pressure from wide cross sections of the population and the Puerto Rican diaspora. The triggering event was a leaked transcript of a Telegraph chat between Rosselló and some of his closest advisors, all men. Rosselló, it should be said, is the son of a former governor, who, like his father, graduated from one of the premiere private catholic high schools here and completed his undergraduate and graduate studies at prestigious stateside universities. A couple of the men in his chat followed similar trajectories. What made the chat so notorious—and damaging to his administration—was its rampant misogyny, classism, and homophobia and, ultimately, his and the group's callous disregard for the suffering of people after the hurricane. The governor and his "brothers," as he described them, were thus outed as the worst sort of *blanquitos*, engaging in offensive—often explicitly violent and even threatening—banter about women, queer, and Black peoples, among others. The protests of that summer—often referred to as a sort of revolution—fittingly shed a light on the racial, gender, and sexual diversity of the Puerto Rican population, as the more traditional—middle aged and male heavy—labor unions and formal political organizations were relegated to the background (LeBrón 2020). After resigning, Rosselló and his family rushed to move and establish themselves in Virginia.

In January 2021, the disgraced governor gave an in-depth interview to the *New York Times*. In it, he speaks candidly about his decision to leave. The interviewer explains:

> He recounted the moment he knew that he would have to leave his $70,000-a-year post: With furious demonstrations swirling in the streets, he and his family, were out in their car when it hit a pothole. His five-year-old

daughter was terrified, and thought they had been hit by gunfire. (Robles and Mazzei 2021)

This comment, as could be expected, garnered considerable criticism. It was read, at best, as a disingenuous and manipulative plea for pity and, at worst, as a callous attempt at rewriting history. I, however, would like to take Rosselló at his word. For the purported truth of his word speaks to his social location as an elite white man, who must now explain how he can no longer live in the place that granted him and secured the privileges that not only shaped his life but afforded him the power to decide over the fates of others, especially in the aftermath of Hurricane María. The truth of white privilege in Puerto Rico, as told by Rosselló, and embodied in *blanquitos* is this: to make a life for themselves in the place of their birth, they, in their minds, must inhabit a place that does not exist. It is a sort of dream-state, if you will, where the hard realities of Puerto Rican life today barely, if at all, register, and when they do, they appear distorted: the sound of a car hitting a pothole is mistaken for a gunshot. The sound of a gunshot, though painfully common in island life, is treated here as exceptional: *this* gunshot is not part and parcel of everyday street violence and crime but rather belongs to an almost unfathomable sort of political violence that made the then first family's continued residence here impossible. In this sense, what is most problematic about the former governor's commentary—and what is more illustrative of *blanquitoness*—is that it seems like, even after two years in office, his most significant encounter with the specificities of life in Puerto Rico was imagined.

This is what makes the figure—*blanquitos*—so laughable, yes. But it is also—as in the case of Rosselló—what makes it so dangerous. Because Rosselló—and those of his same race–class group—do not simply inhabit this place, do not simply flourish in it, but either have the opportunity to govern over the people of the place, or they have the opportunity to draft the dominating discourse about what life is like in the place. Because, yes, depending on the circumstances, a car tire hitting a pothole *can* sound like a gunshot. Because, of course, Rosselló—like any responsible parent—would choose the safety of his children over any other consideration. Because, of course, it would be utterly unreasonable and unjust for his children to suffer on account of the public perception of their father, regardless of how justifiable that perception may be. Because, while Rosselló perhaps deserved to be ousted from the governorship, he certainly—as a husband and father—does not deserve to live in fear of the worst that could happen to his wife and his children.

Here, Rosselló echoes the concerns of the white elite parents Ana Ramos-Zayas interviewed in *Parenting Empire: Class Whiteness, and the Moral Economy of Privilege in Latin America*. For Ramos-Zayas (2020), the emphasis on safeguarding a child's well-being in contexts of extreme social and economic privilege within otherwise precarious societies is a sort of "imperial formation," which both shaped and was shaped by neoliberal public policy agendas and austerity politics. Specifically, for the parents of Ramos-Zayas' study—as for Rosselló—the island place becomes unlivable the moment private security and careful informal vigilance prove no longer effective in maintaining white elite children's innocence. The tale of Rosselló's political downfall—brought on by his own crass mismanagement and demonstrated bigotry—is retold as the story, once again, of an unruly mass of people who have put his daughter's innocence in danger. Never mind that the white father is responsible for both the potholes in the street and ultimately for the alleged unruliness of the people he failed as governor.

And so Rosselló was forced to leave not in response to the political will of the people he once governed, but because whiteness can no longer flourish safely in the island-space. Thus, it would seem, Rosselló is more disappointed with the people he belongs to than he is repentant or humiliated. Like Benny, he too voices his frustration with the average or typical Puerto Rican, who has left him and his family with no choice but to flee, because the only other alternative would be to put the people in a cruise ship and blow them up. Which is something he and his brothers would have, perhaps, gladly joked about in the chat, but that he could not as governor enforce. Of course. And still, there is something to be said about how the mass of Puerto Rican people appears to those charged with the obligation to flourish among them and/ or govern over them. What I am trying to say is that Rosselló can also be thought of as standing in line at the gas station right behind the Venus. One can easily imagine him feeling as if he too had a noose around his neck even as the disasters of the past few years did not claim any of his loved ones; even as, contrary to most islanders who have migrated to the United States, he and his family did not leave on account of real, specific problems related to the availability of jobs, healthcare, and educational opportunities. He too has the noose because this is the one place in the world he can govern, and he much would have loved to rule over a people different from the Venus, whom he perhaps envisions as being so irreducibly different from him but irredeemably tied to him just the same.

I went to preschool with the former governor and graduated from the same high school as one or two of his "brothers." In thinking about his brief stint in public office, the specificities of his historic downfall do not shock me, much less that he made it to the governorship in the first place. The fact is that during his short though storied political career, the running narrative around Rosselló's figure is that he was destined to govern. As such, it didn't much matter how young or how inexperienced he was when he first ran. Nor did his sketchy academic and professional achievements in any way discredited him in his candidacy. His most important characteristic was that he was his father's son; which is what *blanquitos* are always perceived to be: the lawyer son of the renowned attorney father, the doctor son of the esteemed physician, the governor son of the father to us all. While this dynamic is widely and passionately critiqued and ridiculed in diverse forums and settings, social rejection does not seem to be enough to stop the trend in the one area where the people can intervene: in the ballot box.

This strikes me as significant. There would seem to be something about this disavowal of the culture of merit that resonates across Puerto Rican society. Whether it is perceived as a simple matter of putting one's family first, or as a more troubling adherence to a cutthroat, individualist ethics, this particular *blanquito* tradition appears to be embraced by the larger culture. It is, perhaps, another way in which *blanquitos* belong.

To press on this matter further, perhaps then what disgusts people—on the street and social media—of the all too frequent cases of nepotism or corruption in the public sector, involving relatives, friends and/or classmates of the powerful, is not the fact of power being wielded this way, but of the relative powerlessness of their own relationships and connections. There is a saying *necesito una pala* (local slang for I need a hook up) that is used as much, or more, than Arroyo's *yo sé de dónde tú saliste* (I know where you came from). Common sense dictates that it is impossible on the island to procure any job or position without knowing somebody with influence who can tip the scales in your favor. It just so happens that for *blanquitos* the positions include the governorship. Viewed from this perspective, everyday life on the island is a struggle between those that seek to hold you back by holding the perceived shame of your birth, due to race and class, and those who can wield their influence to help you bypass the set process or requirements for any given job or position.

This is, perhaps, what—in my reading—most bothers the white man in Rinaldi's painting about the Venus of Octane. She is on the lookout only for herself, in the same way *blanquitos* pursue their own interests even within the public sector. The difference is the Venus does not have that kind of *blanquito* access. What she has is her body to put in line in front of the white man with a noose for a tie and her *two* gas cans. What bothers the white man is that he is forced to make the same line. What bothers him is that his world seems to be on the verge of apocalypse, and she seems to be flourishing. But what is most perturbing, from a sociological perspective, is that it took a category 4 storm to strike a precarious island colony in the Caribbean for this man and this woman to find themselves waiting in line at the gas station. What's perturbing is that *blanquitos* looking out for themselves leads to despair and death across the island population, while the Venus looking out for herself leads to somebody in line getting upset. In either case, the Venus is the one who bears the consequences: she is likely the one who loses loved ones to botched recovery efforts, *and* she is the one at fault amid the disaster for looking like she's flourishing with two gas and a cell phone.

One last thing about the Rosselló scandal. The presumed mendaciousness demonstrated in the interview does not deny the profound insight to be found in his words: so much of the unsustainability of life in Puerto Rico today is latent in that simple anecdote of a family riding in their car, hitting a pothole, and mistaking it for a gunshot. Chances are the next scene is of the family at the airport—like Rinaldi's *Sons of María*—looking to try their luck in the United States. It is a typical Puerto Rican tale of today, only it doesn't seem right for Rosselló to tell it. Just like it didn't seem right for Fernando to complain about being addressed in English by resort employees. In offering this simple tale as the real reason for his family's departure, Rosselló is claiming that he too has a right to speak and be spoken to in the true language of this place, which is precarity, unsustainability, desperation. It's possible that life conditions here are so grave that these feelings can sometimes besiege even the whitest and most elite among us. It's possible that this is the one aspect of life here that *blanquitos* do not have to imagine, for even they, given the circumstances, can experience *some* level of insecurity and/or uncertainty. It's possible, sure. But the truth of the matter is that potholes are so ubiquitous in Puerto Rico you're bound to hit one on the way to even our most exclusive resorts.

9

Assorted Lessons on and around White Privilege in Puerto Rico

The Puerto Ricans Students Association at my Florida university invited a *bomba* (traditional Afro Puerto Rican musical genre) group from back home to perform at an annual "cultural night." In my attempt at casual banter prior to the performance, I tell the singer I went to high school with a kid with the same last name as his. He looks me up and down and says, "There are black Catalás and white Catalás. I'm guessing your classmate was white, right?" I nod, reluctantly. "We're not related."

It's a Saturday at home and I'm waiting to be picked up by an elementary school friend. It's his birthday and my parents have given me permission to go to the movies with him. My friend shows up at the door with his father. My father goes to greet them while I fetch my present. A few minutes later, they have left without me and I'm told *we* are going to the movies instead. He was one of two, maybe three Black boys in my class.

I'm president of the Puerto Rican Studies Association. Most members are Florida-born Puerto Ricans. Island-born students do not come to many meetings. Something about the way the members seem so intent on "flaunting" their identity. I look, sound, and dress like my fellow island-born students. My fellow members in the association look, sound, and dress like kids my age in Puerto Rico, whom I never went to school with, nor hung out with, nor ever really coincided with anywhere, outside of maybe the mall or the airport. I try not to think about that as I try my hardest to thicken my Spanish accent.

It's 1990 and Mike Tyson is on the TV at my uncle's house. My dad makes the same joke he makes whenever he's watching a boxing match and the circumstances allow for it: *yo le voy al negro* (I'm rooting for the Black guy). Everybody in the house, no matter who was fighting or what championship was on the line, was white. The next morning, a Sunday, we headed over to the basketball court for our customary game of one on one. Every time my dad would make a hook shot, he yelled, "Kareem Abdul Jabar." Every time he snatched a rebound from me, he snarled, "Moses Malone." The courts were on the grounds of a members-only country club. I never saw anybody remotely similar to Kareem or Moses or Tyson set foot on the grounds there. I doubt I would have been allowed to play with them.

It's 1999 and Felix "Tito" Trinidad is fighting Oscar de la Hoya on the TV. The house is packed with island-born Puerto Ricans in Florida. Everybody there is as white as Oscar, but we're all cheering for Tito. Tito's haircut and skin tone resemble those of the Florida-born Puerto Ricans who, I figure, must be crowding another living room in a house near campus yelling at the screen. You could say both groups of students are equally proud, but separate. You could say Tito means as much to the island-born kids as Moses Malone meant to my father. More, even. You could even speculate that there was at least a decent chance that kids from either group had the same last name. Trinidad, even. But you would also have to say that they likely weren't related.

On day one I gave a job talk based on my dissertation research. The second day of my campus visit was to be spent in one-on-one meetings with faculty members. I was interviewing for a tenure track job at the sociology department of a large public, research-extensive university in the northeastern United States. The second sit-down was with one of the longest tenured professors. Meetings were slated to last half an hour. I was supposed to wait for my graduate student escort to lead me from one office to the next at the scheduled time. We were done in less than ten minutes. In the first minute the esteemed professor told me he "didn't much care" about my research. I understood it to be a commentary on my method. I had written a qualitative dissertation and he was a numbers man. So, I tried to explain my methodology, as well as the larger context and possible implications of studying racism among Puerto Ricans at that juncture. He stopped me after a couple of minutes. "I just don't care for who or what you're studying." It was a problem of people, not methodology. We sat in silence for a minute or two, then he got up, stepped into the hall. He came back with my student escort who said I had time for coffee before my next sit down.

The summer before my parents' divorce, they took out a loan to pay for a special summer program at an elite boarding school in the northeastern United States. A couple of my classmates were going. Once there, I met a dozen or so of islanders from private schools like mine. I remember I took French with a few of them and the teacher, a white American woman, could not stand us speaking Spanish in the hallway prior to class. I remember going on a bus trip to see the Boston Red Sox play. I remember a rumor that a couple of white kids from Brazil got rocks thrown at them for speaking Portuguese in town. I remember a white kid from Mexico telling me "us greasers and spics have to stick together." I remember feeling jealous of his perfect English. I remember making one Black friend. I remember she had braids in her hair, which the Puerto Rican girls—mostly blonde—secretly made fun of. I remember going to an end-of-the-summer house party back on the island, all the girls from the trip had gotten braids.

All the Black kids in my high school class seemed older. They were presumed to be on scholarship. They all seemed to have the same haircut. Of course, all the white kids had the same haircut too. Among us, I mean. Another difference was that while not all the white kids had cars, all the kids that had cars were white. Plus, most of them lived nearby. The school was right outside an exclusive, gated San Juan suburb. They could have walked to school. They still drove, though. Otherwise, they had somebody—mother, father, hired help—to drive them. Some of the Black kids took the bus. I don't think I've ever had to take the bus in Puerto Rico.

On one of my first-ever teaching evaluations from a social problems course I offered as a graduate student in Florida, somebody wrote, "The professor has no business in this school, nor in this country." Another wrote than my "look" was "too greasy." I got compliments on my English, though. A student wrote that it was pretty decent, for a Mexican.

I read *The Autobiography of Malcolm X* and *Down the Mean Streets* by Piri Thomas in tenth grade. White schools—even those in the colony—have the best libraries.

I've donned blackface twice in my life. Once, at a family gathering, an aunt got all the boy and girl cousins together in a room. I was ten years old. She had us stand in a line and proceeded to apply black makeup on each of our faces. A popular rap song was playing in the background. We were supposed to memorize the chorus, but we already knew the entire song by heart. When she was finished, she escorted us out of the room and told our parents, uncles, aunts, and adult first, second and third cousins to gather around us. Then she hit play and urged us to sing along. It was over quickly. We were celebrating somebody's birthday.

When the decision was made to restrict public access to the neighborhood I grew up in, they put a small wooden checkpoint that barely fit a desk chair on the sidewalk at the very end of my street. The private security guard had to sit sideways with his legs sticking out toward the pavement. There was a manual gate right in front or right behind the small cabin. Sometime later, the neighbors' association invested in a larger cement structure and an electric, beeper-operated gate. I'm trying to picture that initial structure and its surroundings. I have no idea where the people from the private security company went to use the bathroom. I do remember how we would all get upset when a new guard would stop our car to ask for our name and information, instead of immediately opening the gate for us to pass.

The second time I wore blackface I was a freshman in college. And I was aware of what I was doing. But everybody—meaning my white Puerto Rican, Venezuelan, and Columbian classmates—was doing it. So, I opted in. Privilege is, often, a decision. I don't remember if the memory of the birthday party back home arose while one my classmates was putting makeup on my face. I remember we went to a "Latin night" at a local club. We stood in a circle in the middle of the dance floor and urged each other to sing along.

Whenever news broke in the neighborhood that somebody's house had been broken into, the unknown perpetrators were always presumed to be friends or family of the people who worked in the neighborhood: handymen (mostly male, Black, and Dominican), domestic workers (mostly female, Black, and maybe Dominican), and security personnel (mostly male, Black or coffee with milk or tanned, and Puerto Rican). Most of these people were often referred to as good, decent, hardworking people. They just *happened* to be part of not so good, or decent, or hardworking people.

Because my father was a supreme court justice, officers from the local state police precinct were supposed to come by the house regularly during the day and "look around." They would step out of their cars, pull up their pants, fiddle with their belt, and walk over to the open car port. There was little flip box on the wall with a sign-up sheet. They were mostly male and white or Black or coffee with milk and Puerto Rican. No one ever suspected them of anything.

It's 1992 and my father's assigned government car is outfitted with a siren and loudspeaker. The two young male marshals who are tasked with his— and our—protection are my two closest friends. They are mostly charged with driving him—and us—around, picking up milk and bread at the supermarket at my father's request. They also do a lot of waiting around in front of the house for him—and us—to come out and get taken somewhere. I spend most of my free time sitting with them under a large tree in the front yard. My dad often tasks them with taking me places, mostly to afternoon and night baseball games during Puerto Rico's winter league season. We arrive early so I can hunt for players' autographs. I remember thinking it was a cool job: they got to drive a car with a siren and loudspeaker. They got to have a gun. They got to sit under a tree and go to baseball games with a thirteen-year-old. They were around twenty-seven years old at the time. They had families expecting them at home. We were supposed to address them by their last names. I don't think my father even knew their first names. But they were my friends, so we even had nicknames for each other. Or, rather, I had nicknames for them. One of these referenced a large cartoon bear that a local bank used in its advertisements. It's what I would call my Black friend.

There was a local catcher who wouldn't approach the young fans waiting for him until he got finished his warm-up routine. Upon emerging from the dugout, we would yell out to him to come over, and he would always yell back, "I have to go to work first." I remember thinking he was snobbish. In my mind, it wasn't really work. He was just getting ready to play. I remember thinking that too was a great job to have.

My dad and I often sat at night to watch major league baseball games on TV. Mostly the Mets and Braves. If both the pitcher and batter happened to be Black, which was rare, he would crack the same joke he made during boxing matches: I'm rooting for *el negro*. He referred to most white players by the name on their jerseys.

I remember the two marshals casually referencing having other jobs. I remember they came from the same—or similar—places that my favorite local ball players came from. The more I think about it, it's possible that neither of them cared much for baseball.

I was in ninth grade when Wiso G's debut album came out. It was the first underground rap record distributed by a major label. Wiso had been a student—on scholarship—in the Jesuit school. The rumor was he got suspended in eighth grade. He was two years older than me. The back of the CD case showed him with a gun in his hand.

The first time I held a gun in my hand I was in seventh grade. After months of pleading, I had convinced one of my father's marshals to let me hold his. He took the clip out and handed it over. We were sitting under the tree in front of my house. I held it sideways like US rappers did in their music videos. I had to give it back quickly as the patrol car pulled up in front of the house for the scheduled surveillance stop.

My dad also had a gun. He wore it to work every day. At night he kept it on the floor under his side of the bed. At times, having just arrived home at the end of the day, he would leave it atop the refrigerator and forget about it. It would have been much easier for me to just grab his, but part of me was aware of the possible benefits of claiming a shared responsibility for the event.

I remember after gym class one day a conversation about who among us had ever seen or held an actual gun. One of the scholarship kids said his older brother had one. The kid had a haircut like Wiso's. He also had darker skin than most of us. He didn't explain how or why his brother came to have a gun. I remember thinking immediately, though, that the meaning of a gun in his house was somehow different from the meaning of the gun in mine.

One afternoon, on the way to a ball game, a car suddenly cut in front of us in the expressway. It was a beat-up compact, with five older, darker kids riding. They had the windows down and the music blasting. The marshal switched lanes and caught up to them. He gestured angrily with his left hand. The kid in the passenger seat looked over, stretched out his arm, signaled a gun with his forefinger and thumb, and laughed. The driver started to speed away. I turned on the speaker system in the government car, hit the siren and, in my most grown up and menacing voice, demanded they pull over. They did. We stopped the car right behind theirs. I told them to turn the engine off. We waited a bit and then as our car creeped slowly by them, I signaled a gun with my right hand and laughed. With my window up.

Sometimes I get asked if I'm Italian. A bunch of people take me for Middle Eastern. It becomes stress-inducing after 9/11. I'm in my last year of graduate school and I have a visiting instructor position at a regional state university in Florida. My then partner and I recently moved in together. She's white. As in white American. Her aunt and uncle live close by. My mom flies over for a visit. We all go out to dinner at an outback restaurant. My mom's telling the story about the time she attended the wedding of a former governor's daughter. She's looking to impress them. Because they're white. As in American. They're retired postal workers and have never attended the wedding of the son or daughter of a high-ranking government official. At the beginning of the dinner, I could tell my mom was a little intimidated. By the end, the aunt and uncle were visibly uncomfortable. By then, I had already been living for more than six years in Florida. Still, waiters and waitresses always asked where I was from.

One of my classmates from the Jesuit school also went to Florida for university. We weren't friends but coincided in weekend parties and tailgates. He was white, like me, but spoke English like Al Pacino in *Scarface*. Still, he made a bunch of white American friends. At some point, during sophomore year, I spotted him wearing a T-shirt emblazoned with a confederate flag across the chest. When he would drink too much, he would drape himself with the Puerto Rican flag and tackle trash cans. He liked to refer to himself as Captain Puerto Rico.

At some point I got really into *bomba*. I wanted—but never dared to buy— an *Africa habla en mí* (Africa speaks through me) T-shirt back home. I had Michael Jordan shoes, shirts, caps, and shorts, though. Everybody at the country club wore those.

Though graduates from the Jesuit school often went to the University of Puerto Rico, the expectation was that we would at least attempt to get into a stateside school. Preferably a "good" one. Then again, just going *away* for college was understood to be good. I remember one of my best friends only applied to the University of Puerto Rico. I remember looking at him funny, unable to understand, thinking that he was not taking full advantage of something or throwing something away. That something was understood to be opportunity. But, in actuality, it was whiteness. Coming back from the United States after school made you (more) white somehow.

Sophomore year in college, the Puerto Rican Students Association has invited three—white and male—representatives from the three major political parties in Puerto Rico for a debate on the status of the island. A painting by then graduate student, and now renowned artist, Miguel Luciano is on display at the back of the lecture hall. Then senator Kenneth McClintock—scheduled to make the case for statehood—is examining the painting closely. We are all holding a chuckle as his eyes meet the cartoon-like drawing of Uncle Sam with a large microphone-shaped penis, into which a dark-skinned man in a suit, wearing a white mask, is talking. Most everybody in the lecture hall is white. Most everybody in the lecture hall is Puerto Rican.

I have no idea how McClintock interpreted Miguel's painting. But it did not stop him from standing at the lectern, microphone in hand, and making a passionate case for why Puerto Rico should become a state.

A queer feminist theorist and activist publishes an article denouncing anti-Black racism and white privilege. In her article, she refers to herself—a white woman—as antiwhite. A Black professor publishes a scathing response, where she accuses the white woman of at best naiveté, and at worst of centering white people and co-opting the experiences of people of color. She asks the white woman, in a tongue and cheek way, what she thinks might happen if she—as a visibly Black woman—were to publicly identify as antiwhite.

When discussing racism in class, I often tell students that to be an antiracist is to be antiwhite. Students often look at me quixotically. And so, I clarify, I don't mean that you have to be against white people, but against the idea that whiteness makes people, places, things somehow better. I always leave the classroom thinking I could have made the distinction more clearly, and vow to do so the next time. But I never feel like I do an adequate job.

Classrooms are, by far, the most racially diverse spaces I enter in my day-to-day life. This is not necessarily a commentary on the diversity of the student body at my school but on how anything more than two or three Black faces in a crowd makes me become cognizant of race. The public relations office is also aware, I think. As the school is one of the few that features young Black people in their print, online, and television advertising.

Most of my students come from the same places my favorite ball players came from. I often wonder if I have any business talking to them about racism and white privilege; if my naiveté shows, or worse, if just by stepping inside the classroom and starting a discussion on whiteness, I am, in effect, centering the experiences of the privileged. Furthermore, might I not be now, as I'm writing this, co-opting their experiences?

I am antiwhite. I think it's important to state it publicly, to come up with ways to enact it. I am unsure if this brief, race-conscious accounting of my life might in any way be useful to both individual and collective efforts of antiracist thought and practice. It does for sure make one thing clear: the fact of me being white—even if that whiteness has not always translated well while in the United States—has proved more central and consequential in my life than the fact of me being Puerto Rican.

10

Whiteness for the Rest of Us

Few writers have broached whiteness and white privilege in Puerto Rico outside of the *blanquito* construct. Those who have *have* turned to autoethnographic writing, to intriguing results. The first, best-known and most influential of these is Salvador Vidal Ortiz's 2004 article "On Being a White Person of Color: Using Autoethnography to Understand Puerto Ricans' Racialization." Though focused on the author's experience as white Puerto Rican in the United States, the article does offer important clues regarding the social construction of whiteness and white privilege on the island. Paradoxically these clues become available to us readers even as the author attests to his inability to do so. Vidal-Ortiz writes, "I cannot present accounts of my experiences growing up in Puerto Rico (the first twenty-five years of my life) because my most recent experiences with U.S. racialization taint any possibility of a just representation of racial systems on the Island" (2004: 182). The author wrongly insists in this notion that his experience in the United States, while making the multifarious manifestations of racism anywhere more visible, ultimately serves to "blur" his vision when considering racism as a social phenomenon on the Island. Though I understand the author's concern with the purity of his vision, I would argue that there is no single facet of Island life that is exempt from American influence and ideology. American racial ideology permeates Puerto Ricans' daily life without islanders having to migrate and settle in the US mainland. This by no stretch of the imagination means that the American and Puerto Rican racial imaginary are the same, but it does mean that there is no such thing as one's perspective becoming polluted by American race thought. Thus, I would like to highlight two key instances in Vidal Ortiz's article that prove illuminating for our exploration and understanding of the workings of race and racism on the Island.

In the first of these instances, Vidal Ortiz offers readers a glimpse into the angst of whiteness as it plays out in the most intimate settings of his life. He writes:

> My partner and I lay in bed one morning, at his house; I can hear the river right outside the bedroom window. His and my skin contrast each other— his, a dark brown tone that at times I know I envy; mine, a pale one that shines next to his body ... I bring up the paleness of my skin, since it is almost inevitable to notice my skin color pressed at his. This skin color has often materialized for me body image issues, because at times it renders how I see myself in the world, invisible. Yet that is a struggle for me: to peacefully live within *my* skin. (2004: 184; emphasis in the original)

Here, in remarking on the contrast in skin color between his partner and him, the author intimates that he perceives the color difference—and perhaps color difference in such physical and emotional proximity—as somehow remarkable. This commentary strikes me as significant insomuch as Puerto Rican racial ideology is premised on the un-remarkability of color difference in all aspects of social life, including our most intimate and private settings. Thus, a certain breakage with the dominant ideology is alluded to here. This is further augmented in the above passage as the author goes on to comment on the angst he feels due to his light skin tone. Whiteness here weighs heavily upon the white Puerto Rican. In the author's telling, his skin color renders him invisible. Though he does not elaborate on this feeling, the invisibility and its corresponding angst is not—or at least not fully—part and parcel of his experience in the United States, where, as Vidal Ortiz documents in the essay, he often stands out because of his name or his accent. The invisibility he alludes to here would thus seem to be tied to his experience on the Island. In this fashion, Vidal Ortiz would seem to suggest that there is such a thing as white Puerto Rican experience and that this experience has discrete effects upon white islanders' psyche. This is important insomuch as it not only signals to breakages with the dominant ideology of the supposed irrelevance of skin color on the island. But also because it directly points to an awareness of whiteness in Puerto Rico that potentially extends beyond *blanquito* circles.

In the second instance, Vidal Ortiz shares a potentially failed attempt at explaining the differences between the workings of race and racism in the United States and Puerto Rico:

It is the summer of 1999. I am at a Centers for Disease Control and Prevention (CDC) training as a consultant. A CDC staff person—an African American woman—pulls me aside ... She tells me that she has been to Puerto Rico, and seen the work against HIV infection on the Island. She pauses and then adds: "I just don't see why black folks there aren't organized separately." I try to explain to her that "race" as black and white is very "American" and that folks there have a different racial formation and perhaps racial identification. She has a blank look on her face, as she greets me and walks away ... The experience leaves me with a sour taste: Am I biased in stating that not everyone sees "race" the way *United Staters* do? Was my interpretation of the understandings of "race" in Puerto Rico an unrealistic one? (2004: 186; emphasis in the original)

His interpretation is not unrealistic insofar as it very much reflects, again, the historical and still dominant ideology as it pertains to race in Puerto Rico: there is no need to (divide) and organize islanders based on color insofar as color is not a significant enough social factor in determining people's quality of life. This is not factually true. But it is generally understood as a social fact. What is particularly intriguing and insightful in this instance is the demonstration of doubt and uneasiness with the explanation offered. An uneasiness, I would argue, that corresponds to the angst that his white skin causes him. If in fact Puerto Ricans would not see race as meaningful in some way, then the author's light skin color would not be cause for concern, nor would he be second guessing himself as to whether his rendering of how race works in Puerto Rico was unrealistic. Thus, while Vidal Ortiz, in his autoethnography, states that his interests lie in theorizing the raced effects of white and light-skinned Puerto Ricans on the mainland, what lies in the background is the question of how "settled" are his individual, and our collective, coordinates of race, racism, and whiteness in Puerto Rico. It is my contention then that these two moments in Vidal Ortiz's probing autoethnography open the door to the sort of questioning needed to rigorously explore the workings of whiteness and white privilege on the island.

Following Vidal Ortiz, I would like to comment on three more recent autoethnographic texts on and around whiteness in Puerto Rico, two originally written in Spanish by island residents and one penned in English by a Puerto Rican in the diaspora. In commenting them, I will attempt to tease out from each distinct pieces of insight into the understandings and workings of whiteness as an identity construct and as a social force on the island.

In a thoughtful, moving article, written in the immediate aftermath of the murder of Michael Brown in 2014, and in response to the racist speculation surrounding the African American teenager's moral character, Harry Franqui-Rivera (2014) engaged in an exercise of embodied theorizing on whiteness and white privilege in Puerto Rico. The author acknowledges the novelty of his proposition, writing:

> I'm Puerto Rican. This may startle you. But, since I was born and raised in Puerto Rico, I enjoyed white privilege. My family, for all intents and purposes, socioeconomic and culturally, was a Caribbean mulatto one— though many of my siblings may disagree (we roll like that in the Caribbean) … But it was my very light skin, freckles and copper hair (a trait from that abuelo I never met) that closed the deal. My relatives, neighbors, teachers and even the cops presumed me a good boy, smarter and more handsome than my relatives and peers, and destined to have a bright future because of my complexion, which made me white in el barrio.

He goes on to offer a critical race reading of several events from his childhood and adolescence where he could clearly identify different, markedly better treatment from others on account of his light skin color: the author was complimented on his looks, lauded for what surely would be a bright future ahead of him, protected by the police. Franqui's critical recollections here are important for several reasons. First, they locate the influence of white privilege beyond the notorious spaces of socioeconomic privilege discussed in previous chapters. Second, insomuch as the events reviewed here are of a quotidian sort, the reader gets a sense of white privilege as woven into the fabric of everyday life on the island. And third, insomuch as what he's recounting are other people's reactions to him, it becomes clear that white privilege is not something that an individual can simply call into existence, but rather it owes its existence to larger social dynamics that are beyond any one person's control. Now, these are not startling discoveries in sociocultural contexts where race and racism as systems have been scrutinized over time, but in Puerto Rico, Franqui's focus and findings can be read as new.

Where the author runs into trouble, perhaps, is in presuming that white privilege is only present where he has now opted to see it. The article, for example, starts off asking readers to consider a fake picture of Brown that had gone viral on Facebook. In it, a young, Black male appears smoking what many presumed to be marihuana. Franqui's contacts had shared it as proof that the shooting was justified. In order to denounce and debunk the racist frame at play here, he includes in his article a picture of him as a young man, apparently drinking from a bottle of rum, and describes another:

> In another, I'm posing shirtless with some seven thousand dollars in my hands, lighted cigarette in my mouth, as I do what by any account would be a gangsta pose. I guess I was doing what many people growing without any money would do—even if the money was not theirs. (It wasn't, by the way. It belonged to my brother and two of his friends who had just sold their old boat.) So you see, pictures can be very deceiving. In those two pictures and countless others, I look like a troublemaker or, according to some, a thug—if we are to judge by comments in media.

These two images are then contrasted to a picture of him, several years later, in his military uniform. He closes this reflection asking, "What saved me from being gunned down by the police or from spending my life in and out of jail?" While certainly well-intentioned, the analysis is misguided in that Franqui presumes that because of the similarity in appearance of Brown's picture and his, that Puerto Rican onlookers would essentially see the same thing in each: a thug. In doing so, he is, unfortunately and inexplicably, removing whiteness as a quintessential element in the analysis. The logic would seem to be that the cash or the liquor cancels whatever effect the race of the photographed subject might have on onlookers. If so, this logic is faulty. In looking at Franqui's picture, I see a white kid at a house party. Perhaps the house is not in the nicest part of town, but not in the *wrong* side of town. Perhaps he is up to no good (maybe it's a week night, maybe he's not of legal age to consume alcohol, maybe there are others around him doing the same or worse), but there is nothing in the image that communicates to me that he might be anything other than "good." As such, there is no disconnect, at least in my eyes, between this picture and the one where he is posing in his military uniform. Whiteness as an orientation is pointed toward future success and stability (Ahmed 2006).

Thus, the real wonder would be if that later image of him would not reflect the professional goals and high moral standards one would expect him to meet.

Similarly, his second misstep has him marking a definite, geographical limit to his white privilege. Towards the end of his piece, and reflecting on his experience in the United States, he affirms, "I felt free when I lost my white privilege on the mainland. I guess that in itself is a privilege." The underlying logic here is that entry into a social–cultural context where he does not properly classify as white and thus may be subject to discrimination effectively cancels the white privilege that shaped and formed his life on the island. This logic, again, is faulty. Privilege is not so much lost as the white Puerto Rican migrant might find himself at a loss in the United States, where occasions will arise where he will not be able to pass for white. However, there can always be occasions where he will successfully pass. I want to say that this variance is in itself evidence that white privilege has not been lost so much as it experiences sudden, and at times even dramatic, shifts in translation. Any time that one may have even the slightest chance of passing, privilege is at play.

Lastly, what causes me even more concern is Franqui's treatment of white privilege as a sort of burden migration has released him from. Though he does not expand on his sentiment, one is tempted to read it as an admission of guilt. Or, rather, as an absolution from guilt. Individual acknowledgments of white privilege often generate feelings of shame and guilt in the white subject (Diangelo 2018; Sullivan 2019). In Franqui's story, migration, and its corresponding challenges—not least of which is the awkward positioning of Puerto Ricans within the American racial hierarchy—alleviates some of that shame and guilt. It's a terrible paradox: contexts and situations of discrimination offer a measure of relief to the white colonial subject for now he *too* can claim to be living with the pain, as opposed to unwillingly living off the pain, the system inflicts upon others.

Noted cultural critic Miguel Rodríguez Casellas (2012) expands on this line of thought in his essay "Americano." Identifying as a white, lower middle class, gay man the author explores how his light skin color unjustly marked him as foreign on the island (i.e. people would speak to him in English). Taken for an American tourist, or seen as a *blanquito* in quotidian encounters with others, the author denounces how meanings attached to light skin color on the island impose undue burdens and expectations that he could not or was not inclined to meet. However, the author's focus on his personal feelings of estrangement lead him to downplay the connection between light skin color and privilege. Moreover, in his interest to convey to readers just how poorly the "American" or *blanquito* tag he has often assigned reflected his life conditions, island racism—inexplicably—becomes a type of free-for-all in his telling. According to Rodríguez-Casellas, there are discriminatory structures and narratives against whites just as there are discriminatory structures and narratives against Blacks. Thus, he laments, "I didn't choose this narrative, it was imposed on me." Towards the end of the article there are even explicit claims of reverse racism:

> I'm taking a risk here, I know. Discovering race is also discovering racism. To attempt to describe with my present convictions my personal past, as I remember it, is a dangerous exercise. I'm trying to photograph my discovery of difference, which implied a chasm between expectations of race, class and gender. This allowed me to witness the horror of privilege, not on account of having access to it, but because others insisted on assuming I had it. They positioned me in front of that window, not me and I didn't draw it up either. On the other hand, lacking the physical traits of mestizaje makes you suspicious. It's a form of queerness, in a way, especially if you are not part of the class where whiteness is part of the uniform. (Rodriguez-Casellas 2012; my translation)

This last bit is rather counterintuitive. That racial mixture is celebrated on the island as the foundation of our national culture does not mean that physical traits that point to mixed racial heritage—and particularly those associated with blackness—are celebrated as well. *Mestizaje* is white-oriented. Hence, the popular refrain heard by so many of us over the course of our lives reminding us of the need to "better the race" by marrying someone lighter than you. In this sense whiteness is part of Puerto Rico's national uniform. The difference, as it pertains to social class, might be in the way it is enforced, with the upper classes enforcing more strict measures of whiteness that go beyond skin tone, hair texture, and color, but also tracing (and policing) members and prospective members' ancestors (Ramos-Zayas 2020). In the most elite circles then, simply being white might not be enough to pass. But it is necessary, though. That the author personally rejects and even resents this privilege insofar as he feels it has alienated him from the larger, sociocultural context he belongs to, does not negate the fact that it is infinitely better to be spoken to in English because people mistake you for a tourist, than be spoken down to because people take you for Black. That the author fails to even acknowledge this turns his critical consideration of whiteness into a defense of whiteness. After all, if we can all—regardless of our skin color—be hurt by racism, then racism does not actually exist. At least not outside of the most elite circles.

Casellas, it must be said, is not victimized for looking like a German or an American tourist in Condado. He is not victimized for being perceived to be *blanquito* when he grew up lower middle class. He is, of course, made uncomfortable in these instances. Privilege can be a bother, a problem for the bearers. It is not, however, a victim-making predicament. What's particularly vexing about Rodriguez Casellas's approach to race and racism here is its striking similarity to Fernando's lament. While there is a change in social geography— the pharmacy in Condado instead of the luxury resort—the author's discovery of the significance of race in Puerto Rico begins as well with an encounter with a fellow Puerto Rican at his service, who fails to recognize the author as one of his own. The problem of whiteness and its attendant privileges—across social class—is the problem of belonging. White Puerto Ricans may be the proper face of the island, but they have a hard time fitting in among their countrymen and women. Rodríguez Casellas, like Fernando, instead of, perhaps, reflecting on this discomfort, on this uneasiness, immediately transforms it into resentment toward the rest of the Puerto Rican people. Specifically, they transform the discomfort of racial privilege into a harm done to them. But, again, where is the harm of being spoken to like you own the place?

Thankfully, gender and race scholar Roxanna Domenech (2013), in her own autoethnographic writing, emphasizes social formation over personal experience and ends up offering the most moving and theoretically on-point take on whiteness in Puerto Rico. The article, which details the quixotic looks and incredulous reactions she receives when venturing out into public space with here three Black children, showcases two important aspects of Puerto Rican racial ideology. First, the inordinate amount of attention and rude commentary a white woman with her Black children receives on the street signals to the hard limits of *mestizaje* as a founding ideology. A people that conceives of themselves as truly multiracial and multicultural would not regard the author's family composition as strange. The underlying logic is that people, in actuality, do not willingly, in good conscience, enter into interracial relationships. And so, there must be another explanation: youthful rebellion, adoption (as charity). The author explains:

> Hey, it looks like you like Black men! People have yelled at me in line at the supermarket. To some my children seem like an act of defiance on my part. For others an aberration. I got married to and had kids with a black man and discourses on race, sexuality and power pour out of the mouths of our observers.
>
> In some places, I get questioned about where I'm taking those kids. "They're mine," I've had to assure them. Even so they offer me incredulous looks, on certain occasions it wasn't until one my kids called me "mom" that they've let us pass. Once a cashier asked if those kids that were with me were from Hogar de niños. Wherever I go I get stared at and commented on. I try not to pay them any mind, and keep shopping, eating or walking along. (my translation)

Second, proximity to blackness makes the white subject vulnerable to such a barrage of random comments, questions, quotidian affronts, and intrusions into her personal life, that it is tantamount to a sort of policing. Of course, it is important to point out that while the proximity to blackness makes the white subject vulnerable to harassment, the prevailing racial power imaginary is maintained. If it is youthful rebellion, it is she who likes Black men: they wouldn't have access to her if she didn't. If the kids are not her biological children, it is because they're adopted, not because she is their nanny. In this important sense, Domenech manages to do what Franqui-Rivera and Rodríguez Casellas could not: track, highlight, and problematize the meanings and workings of whiteness in Puerto Rico, even as she is negatively impacted by them, without attempting to establish a distance between whiteness as a social construct and her experience as a white Puerto Rican. Unlike Franqui-Rivera, she does not take her experience of racist harassment as evidence of her being relieved or released from her privilege. And unlike Rodríguez-Casellas, her experience of racist harassment certainly does not become proof that racism in Puerto Rico works in both directions. This, I would say, is a choice. To not turn personal, critical considerations of white privilege into tailor-fitted alibies. There is a definite tendency in the literature on whiteness, as it has developed in the United States, to either wallow in the guilt and shame that typically accompanies admissions of privilege or rejoice in the righteousness of confessing to the guilt and shame brought on by a recognition of white privilege. In refusing to do either, Domenech signals to the kind of critical thought necessary to adequately broach the complexities of whiteness and white privilege in Puerto Rico: you need to put enough of yourself in the text to make the larger social processes visible through your story, but also show the necessary restraint to not make the story, principally or exclusively, about you.

If autoethnography is to prove itself as a useful tool for social theory and understanding, it cannot afford to be framed or oriented as a vindication of the beliefs, experiences, and ideas of the autoethnographer. Autoethnography's critical value is not its use of life stories as testimony, but its use of the personal as a site for more engaged and embodied explorations of the social. As it pertains to the study of whiteness and white privilege in Puerto Rico, autoethnographic writing will only be illuminating to the extent that white Puerto Ricans, in their critical reckoning with the ways in which privilege has played out in their life—including the angst and discomfort and ill-fit that social privilege can entail—make the choice to put the interpretation of their social milieu over the reading public's perception of them. To choose differently would be to "taint" or "blur" our perception of the social phenomena we profess to claim to study. We must remain true to the willingness to question, as shown by Vidal Ortiz: "Was my interpretation of the understandings of 'race' in Puerto Rico an unrealistic one?" And true as well to Domenech's intrepid and valiant analysis, even as it positions her in a markedly different social space from the one her children occupy.

11

The Ugliness of Whiteness: Three Variations

"If I had been white back then, I would have bought you in a minute ... Although come to think of it, you're not dark enough to have been a slave." This is what a workplace supervisor allegedly told a student in my class. We were discussing an essay by Afro Puerto Rican scholar Barbara Abadía Rexach (n.d.), where the author attends to the intricacies of race and gender oppression on the island. The class, I should say, is an introduction to a social sciences course, which I decided to structure around autoethnography as a research method and writing practice. Students are thus urged to consider the connection between their individual life experiences and larger social dynamics. For purposes of this semester—and in attention to the increase in local public discussion on matters of race and racism, in the aftermath of George Floyd's murder—a good portion of the assigned reading is centered on race. Students—mostly first years—have demonstrated a willingness to broach the topic in a manner I had not experienced before. Still, this was the first instance where one offered a discrete example of racial discrimination they themselves had experienced.

The student prefaced her telling of the encounter with the supervisor by stating that Rexach was bringing to light a profound truth about race and gender. The truth, from her perspective, and as she intended to illustrate with the anecdote, was that the way antiblackness manifests itself in Puerto Rico is that people "constantly" want to "save" you from your blackness to the point where you can't claim, much less own, it yourself. Thus, what most worried and "enraged" her about the supervisor's comment was not the *if things were now as they were then I, as a white man, could own you, as a Black woman*, it was rather the *I as a white man of good will, am saving you from the constructs and constrictions of blackness today by marking you as not Black enough*. It was the real-life attempt at dispossessing her of her self-definition and not the fantasy of white ownership that "really messed" with her well-being. She understood the perversity underlying his comment to be that she was somehow lucky to pass as not dark enough around him.

The interaction, I think, encapsulates the prevailing discursive structure of racism in Puerto Rico, at least as it pertains to its quotidian, interpersonal manifestations: white people spare dark-skinned islanders from the perceived dangers or scarcity or ugliness of blackness. Of course, that white people feel and acknowledge the need to save their dark-skinned counterparts implies at the very least a tacit acknowledgement that there is something to save them from: be it systemic racism or a constellation of racist meanings and associations surrounding blackness that would make their life—from white people's perspective—infinitely worse and/or that would alter their relationship with their self-appointed white saviors. And so, the logic goes, you're lucky that I don't see—that I don't let you see yourself—as Black. Because then, somebody—possibly even me—would have bought you in a minute.

At present, those interested in interpreting social dynamics on the island from a critical race perspective are very much adept at identifying, highlighting, and interpreting what these events—at the micro or macro level—signify in Black people's lives and/or in Puerto Rico's relationship with blackness as construct. Little attention is given to that tacit understanding among white islanders as to the horrors of white racism and how they regard themselves— individually and as a group—in relation to those horrors. In other words, my student's supervisor seems to be aware of what his social position vis-à-vis her would have been "back then." What remains unclear is how he sees himself in relation to his understanding of the history of racism in Puerto Rico: how are the particularities of his life today a product of who he might have been then? What differences does he perceive there to be in terms of quality of life between being considered dark enough, not dark enough, and white? How does he move across physical and social space among white and Black bodies? How do we locate this man's sense of whiteness? Is whiteness a burden for him? Was he teased as a child for being too white? Has he been mistaken for a tourist in Condado? Does he walk up to the white mother— as white as him—of the three Black children and ask if those are in fact her children? Does he recognize himself as privileged? The privilege to say to a young Black woman, I could have bought you. How does one approach this man's experience of whiteness in Puerto Rico? How does one broach the topic of his privilege within the Puerto Rican context? How do we engage such a person in reflective, critical dialogue?

There was another interview from my dissertation research that struck me on account of its candidness. I questioned participants not only on how race affected their view of certain people or groups, but also of possible sources for how race, in their view, had become a suitable basis for judging others' moral character, intellectual capacity, and so on. The respondent, an eighteen-year-old self-identified "Latino" college freshman, when asked about the origins of his fear of Black males, answered:

> I don't know. Things I've seen, things I've read, things I've lived. Well, not lived but things I've seen in television, things I've been taught. Not that my parents have taught me these things, but things I've learned in different places, things that my friends say. [Q. Like what?] They would say if an *ugly black* comes up to you in an alley, that type of thing. For example, a very common game in my high school was *the ugly black*. You would say *ugly black*. Very strong. When an *ugly black* jumps up at you what you going to tell him? Or if an *ugly black* comes to stick you up? Or an *ugly black* approaches you and asks you for money? Or if one of these *ugly blacks* in San Juan comes to ask you for a cigarette? These kinds of things that your friends say. (Rebollo-Gil 2005: 108; emphasis added)

The self-corrections in the above passage are illuminating. The respondent wanted to answer truthfully, and so he had to clarify he hasn't had a negative experience with a Black person nor have his parents ever taught him to be racist. He has however learned to be racist somewhere, from someone. Learning, in his case, took place in the form of a high school game. The respondent, studied in a well-known, private Catholic institution in Guaynabo City, which he described as an overwhelmingly white space. Hence, the lack of actual lived experience with Black people. In correcting himself, he is—however unwittingly—lessening the credibility of his racist beliefs: they are not grounded in lived experience, they were not passed down by the people charged with his upbringing. They're the product of a singular, stupid game;

one, among the many you would imagine high school kids might play at different stages of their academic development. As such, his investment—one could argue—should not be profound, given so fleeting a source. And yet, just the level of elaboration he reaches in briefly recalling this game gives us a good sense of the lesson's depth.

What strikes me as significant about the game is how, first, it is premised on white-exclusive spaces: blackness appears out of nowhere, a menacing intrusion. Second, blackness demands a direct response from the white subject: *what are you going to tell him?* The imagined encounters, of course, are always violent: if the Black figure appears it is because he means you harm. Because he means you harm, you must react. According to him, the point of the game was to offer a detailed description of how you handle the *ugly Black*. He impressed upon me the desire—within the confines of the game— to put participants at an impossible situation, where they would have trouble responding.

I am intrigued here by the push of these white youngsters in the private school to leave each other speechless in the face of their imagined Black counterparts. It seems this speechlessness is indicative of the larger collective reticence to attend to blackness specifically, and to race and racism more generally. The respondent's anti-Black sentiments cannot be spoken about because he has trouble identifying their origin. The origin, one could stipulate, is the extreme racial segregation in which he grew up, where it was only possible to suddenly, out of nowhere, run into Black people on the street, because they were neither your neighbors, nor your schoolmates. Now, this isn't accurate, of course. White elites in Puerto Rico are in regular contact with the Black people who attend to their kids or clean their houses or perform yard work (Ramos-Zayas 2020). Or they attend to them in a restaurant, hotel, or store. But these are not the ugly Blacks of the game. At least not while they're working in or around elite whites' homes, taking care of them during dinner or at check in. They only become ugly once their presence in white people's lives is not mediated by a service offered. Their purported ugliness thus resides in their otherwise unimaginable freedom: the fact that they're out there, somewhere. That somewhere, insomuch as it is perceived out of anxiety or fear, could be understood as the island whole.

He grabs his face with his right hand. Like a catcher would put his glove over his face when visiting his pitcher on the mound during the game to discuss strategy and keep the opposing team from reading his lips. Only, in this case, the gesture is not meant to occlude but to overemphasize.

The political commentator whose name was just mentioned is Black. It is important to make a note of it. And it's important to mark it somehow, to perform, so to speak: the hand goes over the face. The face is, of course, white. And though the rest of the faces of the people in the group are not necessarily or not properly white, or, at least, not white beyond a shadow of a doubt, the man we are now talking about is darker than all of us. And how we mark that difference in his absence is by the hand that covers the face during a presumably all-white or mostly white gathering.

It's a passing gesture and I'm unsure if it was even registered by others. But I saw it, though it struck me as radically out of place, and unnerving. It also seemed natural, normal, expected. I want to say that this is a gesture of home, of the viciousness of home. It reminded me of an array of similar gestures to mark blackness in all-white or at least non-Black Puerto Rican settings: the two fingers that gently brush against the forearm; the hand placed next to the mouth as if to whisper a secret (the secret of somebody's visible or less than noticeable blackness); the hand that, shaking, answers the query of how Black somebody seems to them; the head that, shaking, refutes another's claim about a third party's blackness.

The body is put to work in primarily two ways: either the physical gesture works as an overkill, to highlight what is being said openly, directly: "The Black one?" Or to signal what dare not be stated publicly: that so and so is Black. In either case this distressing way in which the white body is put to work to identify and comment on absent or distant Black bodies corresponds to the other work white bodies do when in proximity to their Black counterparts: the tensing up, the looking over the shoulder, the speeding or slowing the pace when walking, the crossing over to the other side of the street. White people's gestures in white-only spaces turn their uneasiness with blackness into an intimacy with each other. It very much brings the group together, as the word "Black" is whispered by the speaker who brushes his hand ever so gently across his inner forearm. The feeling is not so much of an illegitimate utterance: we must not speak of racial difference. It is experienced more as a kindness—we wouldn't want anybody outside of the group who might overhear us to think we're talking about them. As such, Black as a whisper, Black as a gesture is supposed to spare others of pain or shame or discomfort: "If I had been white back then, I would have bought you in a minute ... Although come to think of it, you're not dark enough to have been a slave."

In these exchanges at least one important thing occurs. The group acknowledges the underlying social structural framework of their bond. Now, they're not simply friends from school or work or the neighborhood, there is another, more significant, connection between them. Of course, none of them would—and none of us did—in fact expressly acknowledge this. But you—I, in this instance—feel the weight of what is known but left unacknowledged. Or rather, you—I, in this instance—feel the weight of individually and collectively withholding the necessary comment, so that it remains unacknowledged. To speak up in that instance feels like breaking that school, neighborhood or workplace bond. To make such a remark would imply a failure to comply with the terms of our shared sense of belonging. To remark on whiteness is to rescind whiteness however briefly. To create discomfort, or rather, to bring discomfort on to yourself. And so, I didn't.

What these three instances have in common is, precisely, the individual and collective investment in whiteness as a measure of social comfort. My student's supervisor felt comfortable making such a nefarious comment because, in her analysis, he was being generous in his attempt at extending to her a sudden relief from her blackness. Similarly, the "ugly Black" game could be interpreted as a disturbingly candid manifestation of the otherwise unstated comfort of inhabiting an all-white or mostly white space, within a larger and presumably more racially diverse milieu that generates anxiety among white elite adolescents and their families. Lastly, the commitment to secrecy among whites in commenting on another's blackness "out in the open" signals to an individual and collective adherence to a code of conduct in the island as it pertains to race: one must be careful not to bring up what could otherwise hurt somebody else's feelings, or more precisely, hurt our image of ourselves in our racially exclusionary social spaces, which we do not want to openly acknowledge as exclusionary. Because to admit to its exclusionary character is to recognize whiteness and white privilege as a site of agency, as a social situation that individuals and groups help bring about, as opposed to an organic formation.

Whiteness is more comforting in Puerto Rico. Partly because—contrary to the United States—a wholehearted, public embrace of whiteness and its attendant privileges does not require of the bearer to publicly adhere to the discourse of white supremacy. Here, whiteness can and is celebrated and defended vehemently in the unraced terms of the Puerto Rican people and culture, where—from any white islanders' perspective—Black people have a part in. In this sense, whiteness here can exert power without having to resort to hatred or hostility. It's not necessary to hate blackness or Black people, if they are recognized and embraced to a point. The point, perhaps, where the members of a white-only circle lower their voices to speak of a Black acquaintance to not "hurt his feelings" or hinder the group dynamic. The point where a Black acquaintance can be—thanks to the goodwill of the white speaker—saved from her blackness. The point where all the "really Black people" exist only in our imagination.

12

Two Poems

Perhaps the greatest privilege that whiteness confers to people in Puerto Rico is plausible deniability. Because race is, often, presumed to be the last thing, a denouncement of racial discrimination can easily be discredited and dismissed. Moreover, because there is a cultural investment in race being the last thing, other possible factors are not brought up in the discussion as obligatory considerations before taking race into account, but rather they are brought up to avoid entertaining race as a serious possibility. The investment is so great and far-reaching that it can even become an obstacle for those, who, like me, seek to engage in the critical self-reflection and analysis that both autoethnography and antiracism entail.

Below are two poems, written within just days of each other, in the spring of 2021, as I was working on this book. Though they were not meant to be part of this project, I am sharing them here because, when considered together, they shed light on the trappings of studying whiteness in Puerto Rico. In particular, the two texts speak to how what is rightly regarded as a conscious, regular practice of critical race thinking can very much result in the unconscious formation of habits of thought, which allow one to keep seeing (the same) race effects in certain aspects of one's life, as other important race effects remain occluded.

Every White Hand in the Room

On reading Etheridge Knight's *Hard Rock Returns to Prison*
from the *Hospital of the Criminal Insane* in Puerto Rico

I read Hard Rock in Father Gordon's 10th grade English class.
An American Jesuit in the colony, all he had to do
was praise your English to make you feel more special

than all boys in the school. Most of us were white too,
but in the colony, color is trickier or stickier. Plus,
back then, everybody was mostly worried about
who stuck a look on whom in the restroom.

I don't remember how we broached "the role of race" in the poem.
We also read Shakespeare that year and I remember nothing.
But I can hear Father asking for a volunteer to read Knight's poem out loud.
It was the only time every white hand in the room went up.

Always, when I walked into the restroom, I was so worried about being
singled out for sticking a look on somebody, I ended up
stuck on whoever was there. Teachers, especially.

I remember hating Shakespeare and loving Hard Rock.
I remember my English got so good that year,
everybody treated me special.
I remember thinking Etheridge was a girl's name—
the only one we read all year.

Legacies

Carlitos Colón vs. Stan Hansen
[WWC 1987]

Wrestling in Puerto Rico was bloody. And a sin
for me to flinch from Carlitos,
tomato-faced, on TV.

I went to school with Carli, his eldest son,
who became a wrestler too.

*

Once in college I waited in line to buy a shirt
with the face of my middle school friend on the front.

We weren't friends—
I had stuck a cigarette, as you would a pencil,
behind my ear after seeing him do it.

He caught me staring,
wondering what it might feel like
to see your father bleed on TV every week.

My dad would look at the screen and scoff.

*

I never once saw my father bleed. Still,
I could barely stand to look at him without flinching.

*

Carli still wrestles today.
Staring at the screen, I wait
to catch a glimpse of the boy in my memory.

I do the same with men my father's age
I pass on the street. If I flinch,
it's him.

The two poems mine memories from the same period in my life. Race, however, is only salient in "Every White Hand in the Room," as the speaker is intent on making a commentary on how blackness is consumed in elite all-white spaces. In thinking through this poem during the writing process, I made a quick fire inventory of "social facts" about my experience in high school: that it's an all-boys school was obvious upon entry. That (almost) all boys belonged to the upper middle and upper classes became apparent with the passage of time. That it's (almost) all white was never remarked upon, and as the poem documents, seemed to go unnoticed even as (some) key texts by (select) African American authors were consumed as course material. Expected to be good students, we were taught to identify the larger social context the poem responded to. Expected to become good members of our social class, we were never asked to consider our own sociocultural landscape under a racial lens. The strength of the poem thus lies in its denouncement of the school space as racially exclusionary, for making whiteness visible.

This is the sort of poem sociologists—and not necessarily readers of poetry—love because all its purported meanings lie in the surface for quick identification and relatively straightforward analysis: "Color in the colony is trickier or stickier"/ "I remember hating Shakespeare and loving Hard Rock"/ "I remember thinking Ethridge was a girl's name." The school space is rendered in verse in all its dense, yet unacknowledged, devotion to the privileged young white males, whose intellectual acumen and critical thinking skills are to be rigorously developed, but only to the point where the ideological confines of their sense of self and worldview remain unthreatened. In writing it, I was looking to make a definitive commentary about race and racism in Puerto Rico: how, even in contexts where racially exclusionary dynamics were obvious, it remained always just out of view, as questions of gender, class, and sexuality took precedence. The poem, in this precise sense, *works.*

But, really, the truly worthwhile critical race comment can be found in "Legacies." Or, more precisely, around "Legacies." Though there is no mention of it in the text, it was a Black boy I was spying on, and mimicking. Years later, it was a Black man whose face I wore on my T-shirt. Though I have written—at considerable depth—about my "relationship" to both Carlos and Carlito Colón (Rebollo Gil 2018), I wrote and revised this poem over the course of three months, without even giving a thought as to how it too was a "race" poem. Notice, please, the level of emotional investment in the piece, which makes "Every White Hand in the Room" seem almost clinically cold. In contrast, the strength of "Legacies" as a text is entirely affectual: here is the speaker turning to this boy in his class and toward the relationship of the boy with his father, and who in turning toward them is looking to turn away from his own father. Here is this boy who does not outgrow the habit of sneaking a glance at his classmate and years later goes on to buy a T-shirt with his face on it. Here, in summary, is this caring and careful looking that the speaker is doing, and nowhere in the poem does it mention that the classmate and his father are Black. It is as if the turn to look at them in real life, as well as the turn to affect in the poem, could not withstand the *added* element of racial difference.

When thinking about race, my thoughts immediately turn to the markers I, as a sociologist, was taught to focus on: group composition, spatial dynamics, power differentials. But there are other markers I am blind to. In attempting to figure out the emotional coordinates of my relationship with my father, I fixated on a Black Puerto Rican man and his son, but the high emotional investment made race recede into the background, leaving the poet and scholar in me to go look for it elsewhere. As if the fact of whiteness were relevant in the critical consideration of my school as an exclusive physical and social space, but irrelevant when pressing myself to think critically about my selected affinities as an adolescent. But this is not true. The fact of the matter is I loved my English teacher. I was, in many ways, in awe of how he spoke, how his voice overtook the room, how he listened, and how he looked at you—at me—when you managed to say something interesting in class discussion. And yet, I had no problem representing this man as "the American" in the poem, in zeroing in on the colonial framework that shaped his role as teacher and ours as students. I had no problem emphasizing the political—and yes, racialized—dimensions of what feeling "special" meant in the context of the school. Affect is no obstacle to critique in that piece. With Father Gordon I can reconcile the vision of him as a dear teacher with that of the imperial visitor. But with the Colóns I must choose, either they appear in my memory devoid of race as a significant affective referent in my life or they simply do not appear. I can only see my classmate's relationship with his father as a suitable counterpoint to my relationship with my own father to the extent that I ignore the social context to which the four of us belong. This relative critical awareness vis–à–vis selective blindness would seem to suggest that a white person can be very much attuned to the multifarious and ever so subtle ways in which colonialism might play out in everyday life in Puerto Rico—including how colonialism is racialized—and remain oblivious to how notions of whiteness and blackness shape and influence relationships among Puerto Ricans themselves.

The result of this obliviousness, in my case, is a taking. In "Legacies" I plucked my old classmate from the (almost) all-white space of the school featured in "Every White Hand in the Room" and used him and his dad and what they represent in Puerto Rican popular culture for a contextless exploration of my feelings toward my father. By taking racial difference out of the universe of the poem, the (white) heart and soul of it can come through more openly and freely. This—to refer to Rinaldi's painting—is how the heart and soul of whiteness is a noose.

13

How *Blanquitos* Belong, a Reprise

They call it *la Vuelta del pendejo* (the sucker's stroll). Only, it's not really a stroll if you must do it by car. But the island is like that: most everything is close, but you can't reach most places on foot. Sidewalks, if available and in acceptable conditions, are used as parking space for homes and businesses along streets and avenues. So, if it's Sunday afternoon and you have nowhere to go but need to get out of the house, you head over to Old San Juan and Condado, like a sucker.

In Old San Juan it's easy to spot the tourists. They tend to walk in groups of four or more, drinks in hands, in their cruise-ship attire, and sweating profusely as they make their way up and down cobblestone streets. In Condado, you see tourists too, but—admittedly—it's harder to distinguish them from the people who live in Condado. You have to roll down your windows, while stuck in traffic, to catch passerby's conversations. If you hear Spanish, it's a local. If you hear English, it's a toss-up. White Condado residents often speak English among themselves. Or Spanglish. Just not the type of Spanglish that brings up images of the Puerto Rican Day Parade, red eye flights from New York to Puerto Rico. It's the type of Spanglish one can only encounter in select and exclusive spaces: top island private schools, ski vacations in Veil, senior class trips to Ivy League colleges, spring break, upscale restaurants, and ritzy night spots. It's the Spanglish of privilege and as such it is not indicative of large-scale social processes of colonial imposition, social and cultural displacement, and mass dispossession. It is indicative, rather, of ideological, financial, and affective relations with the imperial power, and is thus wielded as a gate-keeping tool: if you can't quite catch the tone or are not familiar with the references you simply don't belong, regardless of how *good* your English-speaking skills may be. What matters is not your proficiency as a speaker, but the social genealogy of your speech patterns. And so, you must hope against hope that the car in front remains stopped just a few seconds longer for you to catch one more turn of phrase before deciding between tourist or local.

In looking at the local white people in Condado, I encounter a different way of embodying whiteness. They seem freer. As a child of gated communities, confidence in your body sets in when walking into other people's houses, no matter the size or splendor; when walking into a store and asking casually, but assertively, to speak with the manager; in walking into an office space or a social club or hotel lobby or an academic institution to carry out whatever business you may have there. But this confidence disappears immediately when you must will your body to move across public space in Puerto Rico. And it is a matter of will, of conscious effort. As a child of gated communities, my body turns tense, increasingly aware of my surroundings, of how I may be perceived. Then other considerations sweep in, as heightened awareness of danger—and thus of reading certain bodies (all Black, or darkened by dress, or movement) as inherently dangerous—starts to overwhelm you and you start to feel bad about yourself and your thoughts. Then, almost as a reflex, you flinch as somebody, unnoticed, brushes by you.

White people in Condado, though as white as me, do not move the same as me, pushing baby strollers down the avenue with one hand, holding a Starbucks cup with the other. They even seem to "forget" themselves in vigorous runs, dressed impeccably as mannequins in storefront windows. As a child of gated communities, I've run like this before, certainly, but from the front of my house to the guard station and back. In looking at them I also notice that this sense of white freedom is not a product of the physical space. While, yes, Condado can very well overwhelm the visitor with its architecture of leisure, wealth, and privilege, it is impossible—today—to not also consider the many abandoned structures that housed restaurants and businesses. It is impossible not to notice the number of people without a home. Condado, in this regard, looks no different from most urban areas on the island. Thus, it occurs to me that what maintains the aura of elegance and prosperity in this place are precisely white local bodies. Tourist bodies don't have this effect, for tourist bodies carry their own tension in a way. People also will themselves to move across foreign space, especially when those spaces are not only foreign, but precarious, peopled by dark or darkened bodies, and therefore understood to be dangerous somehow. A tourist, in this sense is not free. Or not *as* free. It's the body of the white local that brushes past the strolling tourist that gives Condado its aura of luxury amid the copious signs of deterioration all around.

Perhaps this is part of the reason why the privileged whites of Condado look down on the privileged whites of gated communities in Guaynabo (Ramos-Zayas 2020). The gate, in their view, makes their counterparts—who they might know from school, social clubs, and skiing vacations in Veil—less cosmopolitan. Their privilege bears the obvious, ugly mark of *blanquitos'* need for security. Because of the gate, there is no city as such that they and their children can experience. They go from the locked house in the gated community to the locked car which takes them to gated school grounds, or the shopping mall with its private security company, or the restaurants and bars in strip malls with valet parking service and tickets to validate. Certainly nothing like you imagine wealthy New Yorkers' or wealthy Parisians' life, so "out there," in the open.

Whiteness in Condado is different, like Paris and New York are different. It's not that elites here are more cultured. The schools in the area are not necessarily better than the schools in Guaynabo. Plus, the drive to the museum, performing arts center, and music conservatory are short. It's different because it is freer to manifest itself in public. Freer in the sense of the body. It's the body walking that communicates privilege not the brand clothes or the make and model of the car. It's the body exercising across public space, not in gymnasiums or gazebos in gated neighborhoods. It's the absence of the gate, the body that moves as if it does not need to keep the rest of the population at bay to maintain and enjoy its privilege.

Or does it?

14

Black Lives Matter *en español*

There's a Black Lives Matter mural on the roof of the Hiram Bithorn Municipal Stadium in San Juan. There's another painted across the pavement in Condado's Ashford Avenue, right in front of the *Ventana al Mar* (Window to the Sea) plaza. The murals were painted at the behest of then city mayor Carmen Yulín Cruz, in a special collaboration with local rapper and international superstar Bad Bunny. If you want to have a look at the one atop the stadium, you have to catch a plane out and then come back. The one on the avenue is considerably more accessible. It just happens to have been painted in one of the most inaccessible parts of the city. In terms of who can afford to live there, I mean. Or who can afford to go for a stroll in the area without being harassed by state police or private security. In either case, both are infinitely more accessible to tourists flying in and booking a room at one of Condado's many signature hotels. Which begs the question: how exactly do Black lives matter here?

One possible answer was given in a tweet by *Colectiva Feminista en Construcción* (Feminist Collective under Construction) member Shariana Ferrer Nuñez, who wrote:

> Painting BLACK LIVES MATTER on Ashford [Avenue] so the blanquitxs that live in Condado can feel good about themselves. They take pictures from up in their penthouse or with the drone. Those who clean and cook—those who serve them—barely survive the politics of the racial state. (Mercado 2020; my translation)

Ferrer is right. To an extent. For those white, wealthy, and "woke," Black Lives Matter painted in large, yellow letters on the street that runs through your very exclusive and seemingly white-only area quite possibly makes you feel on the right side of history-in-the-making. Moreover, seen from this perspective, it is not so much a piece of street art at the service of a radical ideal (Black Liberation) but rather at the service of power: Condado residents get to live where and how they live, without questioning how the social coordinates of their life might figure in the broader spectrum of Black life in the Americas and still feel like they are all for Black lives by either welcoming the mayor and the rapper's action or by simply putting up with the mural, and not making a fuss about it. Of course, for the latter group, the mural may very well present a problem. Specially given Condado residents' relative isolation from scenes of sociopolitical unrest and collective disruption—the area is free of both important places of government and iconic edifices of finance, which helps shield it from protesters—it might be read by at least some residents, as an imposition and, more importantly, an invitation for the precarious and malcontent to march upon Condado under the banner of Black Lives Matter. In this sense the mural might still, in spite of it all, be at the service of a radical ideal.

Often, what happens with what are correctly identified as attempts of co-optation—whether by the state or corporations—of grassroots oppositional movements, their artifacts and discourse, is that in activists' critique of these gestures, opportunities of creative interventions are discarded. Why, instead of assuming that the mural makes Condado whites feel good about themselves, would one not imagine that they now might feel like their community has just become visible in a political map of the island? Why, instead of assuming that the people who cook and clean will simply continue to toil in their day to day, as if those three words were never there, would one not imagine the possibility of them making those words matter suddenly, dramatically, in their context and circumstance? Why, instead of posting an immediate dismissal of the gesture, would one not publicly, creatively, and dramatically approach the mayor to press her on what concrete steps her administration will take on behalf of Black Lives Matter?

Radical liberatory gestures are generous. They often escape their authors' intent, as well as onlookers' and critics' most obvious interpretations. The generosity, again, is of the gesture, not of the mayor or the rapper. The message of the mural, unbeknownst to Cruz, might exceed her intentions (Jackson 2020). Even betray them. By commissioning the work, Yulín might very well have been appropriating a message, but she cannot control its future uses. What for her might not have been more than a superficial and self-serving embrace of a cause to attract prospective tourists to the capital city during the pandemic can garner not only radically different meanings but also a distinct materiality that would render the Black Lives Matter movement recognizable in Puerto Rico, which would make it responsive to the specificities of our social and cultural context.

The question thus is of considerable importance: how could Black lives come to matter in Condado? What would it look like? In recent years, area residents have made headlines for their investment in private policing efforts (Rivera Puig 2018). Thus, though seemingly an open community—there are no gated neighborhoods—passersby are subject to heavy vigilance on the street, as they walk in or past luxury boutique stores, hotels, and condominiums. What would Black Lives Matter mean in such a space, where the only Black people not in uniform are presumed to be tourists? Furthermore, why not in Spanish? One would presume that flight attendants when asked about the meaning of the words atop the stadium by an interested passenger would be willing to translate. As would the hotel concierge. And so, the installations as executed would seem to denote, on the one hand, as Ferrer rightly notes, a disregard for Afro Puerto Rican peoples, and, on the other, a certain level of fear. That Yulín Cruz, who during her two terms in office made it a point to erase the traces of the previous pro-statehood, English-privileging administration, would opt—in collaboration with a Spanish-exclusive rapper—to stick to the English original is telling. It is as if antiracist struggle has no possible Spanish translation. Or, worse, that the struggle against racism better not find an adequate Spanish translation in the Puerto Rican context.

Still, at the risk of sounding foolish, I want to say that there is liberatory potential for that mural on Ashford Avenue, as it sits in front of a plaza, nestled between the exclusive Condado Vanderbilt hotel and a small strip of eateries. The plaza, with a generous patch of grass where one could ostensibly play with one's dogs, and where children could ride their bikes, used to be the idyllic setting for a monthly series of free jazz concerts, sponsored by Heineken. The series was cancelled some time ago. And it just so happens that neither dogs nor bicycles are allowed on the premises. That's what the private security guard standing right next to the waffle shop will tell you, as he told anthropologist Ana Ramos-Zayas, when she showed up with her son and his bicycle. She writes:

As Sebastián and I approached the park, a young dark-skin security guard approached us, almost timidly, to let us know that "bikes were not allowed in the park." My face must have shown disbelief, because the guard tilted his head and made a facial gesture almost shrugging and agreeing with what I was thinking: How could it be that one of the few green areas with cemented lanes in the neighborhood could forbid kiddie bikes? I felt bad for the security guard, who looked obviously uncomfortable at trying to justify something he viewed as ridiculous. Hesitantly he told me, "They don't want to have an accident of people bumping into bikes ... You know, the tourists and all the new people moving in." (2020: 84)

The author then told one of the participants in her study, an elite white Condado resident, of her encounter:

When I expressed my surprise to Manolo, he was sympathetic but adamant that the no-bike policy was "unfortunately, a necessity." He explained, "This rule was really not directed to forbid young kids from riding their bikes, but unfortunately, that's the byproduct of it. Here in El Condado, we're having an issue with young men from Lloréns [public housing complex, *los muchachitos de Lloréns*] riding bikes, very aggressively and recklessly. They rob, grab cell phones, and when you're with your kids that makes you very vulnerable. As parents, we had to get involved in that." (Ramos-Zayas 2020: 85–6)

And so, while the reasoning for the pet prohibition remains unclear, the prohibition on bicycles is there to keep the area as white and as upper class as possible. The politics of the mural then are an affront to the politics of the plaza and of the surrounding elite community. It helps make visible the racial segregation and surveillance that Afro Puerto Ricans are subjected to. The mural, then, brings some attention to this historically ignored social fact— so long as you can read English, of course. And attention, as they say, leads to awareness, which might bring about eventual social and political change. Perhaps this is what the mayor and the rapper had in mind. Hopefully so.

Still, one would have to wonder about the efficacy of the gesture. What good is the mayor signing off on Black Lives Matter as street art, if a Black Puerto Rican boy in a bicycle can ride by the yellow letters and still not be able to cross through the plaza on the way to the public beach? Of course, the guard who stops him will not tell him that Black boys like him are not allowed. But it will, chances are, be understood that way by both parties. Because, as Ramos-Zayas notes:

> While race is traditionally thought about in terms of people, ultimately and historically, the politics of race become comprehensible only when considered in territorial terms. Thus, race is always, more or less explicitly, the racialization of space and the naturalization of segregation. (2020: 59)

In this precise sense, "no bicycles allowed," as uttered by a dark skin private security guard, is a much more forceful, clear, widespread, socially significant and life-determining message about the state of Black lives in Puerto Rico than whatever mural the mayor could ever commission. It keeps the "social truth" of social segregation and prejudice based on class and race hidden enough for the prohibition to pass as anything but discriminatory, but the truth is close enough to the surface for it to have readymade and community-wide justifications for it.

Thus, in the Puerto Rican case, perhaps a more adequate, and context-specific, and life-affirming, and infinitely more hopeful articulation of Black Lives Matter would be *Los muchachitos de Lloréns importan* (The Kids from Lloréns Matter).

15

Go Home

How's your English? The new neighbor bends to ask our boy. The boy runs back to hide behind my leg. *How about dad, does he speak any English?* He's standing upright now, facing me. I nod.

Our boy knows bits and pieces of songs from his parents' playlists. He knows *parking* and *closet* and *hamper,* and a bunch of other English words we use as if they were Spanish.

The new neighbor is, likely, on a short-term rental. He got fooled by the promise of being fifteen minutes away from the beach, which is true. But fifteen minutes away puts us in the middle of the city.

Come be my translator, he says, like I must have been waiting for this moment where all the English words in my head would finally be of service to ... I can't say he's a stranger, even if this is his first time here and he just got fleeced by a local's entrepreneurial spirit. So, I say nothing. Watch him give up with a shrug and walk away.

The boy does not yet know how silence can be a language. Today he learned *Yankee go home* but not in those terms exactly.

As Covid-19 cases continue to rise, tourists from the United States are flocking to Puerto Rico. You see them, in beach attire, often without masks, moving across Old San Juan and Condado, with no regard for the social distancing protocols in effect. Some are white. Including one woman who posted a video denouncing racism in the San Juan community of La Perla, after receiving a beating at the hands of a female resident. Some are Black. Including those featured in a couple of videos gone viral on social media. In one of them, four Black women, mask-less, are shown dancing on the street in front of La Concha

Hotel in Condado. In another, a group of men and women are kicking and punching a woman who has been thrown or fallen to the floor in the airport.

It's difficult for the white woman in La Perla to garner sympathy. A historically marginalized community, La Perla is as iconic as social cultural referent as its inhabitants have been criminalized and policed by authorities. Most recently, it became a popular tourist destination after it was featured in the video for a hit pop song. The fact of her whiteness can, in the local— particularly left-leaning, de-colonial—imagination, mean that (1) she had no business coming to Puerto Rico in the first place, (2) just because a community looks to profit on its sudden international fame, does not mean everybody's welcome or that anybody can act as they please, (3) Puerto Ricans can't be racist against Americans, (4) at least not against white Americans, and (5) is Yankee go home racist?

The images of the Black tourists are harder to deal with. How are African Americans situated regarding islanders? Is their presence here, as tourists during the pandemic, as problematic politically as that of their white counterparts? Can I call a Black man or woman, Yankee? Can I yell at them to go home? Can I denounce the callous disregard they show for island residents as another quotidian manifestation of colonialism? Or is that racist?

I could, of course, take the easy way out: it's not the individual tourists per se, so much as the racist logic of the system manifesting itself by way of cheap flights to a bankrupt island colony that has no control over its borders, creating the conditions for marginalized people from the empire to revel in the wonders of the colony, which its own residents cannot enjoy due to the lockdown. And yet, it's not the system, drinking on the street, breaking all manner of social distancing protocols, putting others at risk. One should be able to voice the displeasure, the discomfort these events provoke, right?

To complicate matters further, news outlets have also made note of a considerable number of Puerto Ricans from the diaspora arriving on the island for the first time in ten, twenty years, motivated by the prospect of their children setting foot on their parents' homeland, meeting extended family, connecting with their culture. You certainly can't call them Yankees.

But could you at least yell at them to go home?

My interest here is not to sound contrarian. The questions regarding Black American tourists and Puerto Ricans from abroad, though phrased in an admittedly incendiary manner, are sincere. I am interested in exploring the ease with which I, for example, dismissed the white woman in La Perla and the confusion and concern that the images of African American and Puerto Rican visitors provoke in me. My desire is not to figure out what, if anything, I could yell at the latter, but rather what the island space and its inhabitants might be to them, and how we here can and should interpret their presence in this time and circumstance.

My gut reaction is that the three visitors share, to an extent, a common vision of the island: it is a dream space, to be filled by each visitor's fancy. For the white American tourist, the island is, even in times of local economic crisis and global pandemic, an exotic paradise. For the Black American tourist, the island is, perhaps, a welcoming space in times of social and political unrest across American cities in the wake of George Floyd's murder. For the Puerto Rican visitor from the diaspora, the island, perhaps, has not ceased to be— despite everything—the romanticized image of the welcoming homeland. In each of these three scenarios, islanders do not properly exist: service workers exist; the faces and places from the music video exist; family, culture and history exist, but not people stuck in their homes or rushed to hospitals or arrested for protesting or forced to work, or unemployed, or detained by police by daring to act like a tourist in their own country.

In this precise sense all three visitors are Yankees, and they should all go home. Whether they get yelled at or not.

And yet, only one of these visitors induces a panic beyond the fear of contagion. Videos of Black tourists dancing, and fighting were worrisome in and of themselves. The fact is that a couple of weeks prior to the publication of these videos, another fight between tourists in Condado was recorded and shared heavily on social media. In the video two white American men confront each other on the sidewalk. One hits the other over the head with a chair. Upon falling to the ground, a knife slips out of his pocket. The other man grabs it and proceeds to stab him several times in neck and face area. While decidedly more violent, the footage of this incident did not provoke the same level of consternation. Black tourists have been a cause for concern. Government officials, avoiding any race-specific language, have spoken publicly about how—due to the drop in prices—the island space is receiving *a different group of tourists*, one that, perhaps, is not accustomed to visiting another country. Black tourists, then, though catered to because ultimately the frail local economy *needs them*, are viewed here in a similar fashion to the Venus: *They do not know how to act. How could they not know how to act? Their acting up like that is getting in the way of our collective flourishing.* Their presence, in this regard, is further illustration of the grave conditions the island finds itself in. That it has no choice but to put up with them now, in the worst possible scenario, in much the same way that Rinaldi's businessman had no choice but to put up with the Venus—so oblivious to the surrounding context—ahead of him in line. Only it's not her—or their—obliviousness that is the major problem. It's just the fact that she/they is/are ahead.

In this precise sense, only the white tourist is a Yankee. And only he can be told to go home. Because he is the only one that has a home. The rest of the characters involved—Black American tourists, Puerto Ricans from the diaspora, and islanders—inhabit certain spaces and move in between others, making a claim on a particular place and on their right to move between places. But these claims never go unchallenged. As such, neither their attempts at place-making nor their travels are ever safe. This does not mean that they, as individuals, are not responsible for their actions, but it does demand that we call them by the appropriate names when we demand that they go back to where they came from.

Fellow dispossessed, go home.

16

Erasure

On July 26, 2020, the *Movimiento Socialista de Trabajdores* (Socialist Workers Movement) staged a protest in the vicinity of Puerto Rico's lone international airport. Early in the day, police established a checkpoint on the access roads. By the time the caravan of protesters arrived, authorities prevented them from getting anywhere near the facilities. As some protesters stepped out of their cars onto the avenue, a confrontation took place, which led to one of the organizer's unlawful, unnecessarily forceful arrest. Fortunately, he was released shortly after arriving at the nearest precinct (Costa, 2020).

Protesters were calling for inbound flights to be cancelled to curtail increasing levels of contagion from US tourists. Video of the arrest was widely shared, and the incident was picked up by local media outlets. What was not remarked upon, however, was that the video shows the mostly white arms and hands of police officers pressing down on the chest, shoulders, and face of Ricardo Santos, who is Black.

Protestors returned to the airport on August 9. A banner read *nuestras vidas antes que sus ganancias* (our lives before—or over—their profits). I stared at the livestream wondering *whose lives exactly*. The protest again was staged by the Socialist Workers Movement, in conjunction with the de-colonial, anti-austerity activist group *Jornada se acabaron las promesas* (No More Promises). Obvious answers would be workers' lives, Puerto Rican people's lives. However, it's hard not to consider the wording of the slogan in relation to Santos's unlawful arrest weeks earlier: Why Not Our Black Lives? The banner read like a missed opportunity, at best. And at worst, like an erasure. As if the previous demonstration had simply resulted in a random arrest. As if Santos was not particularly vulnerable to, and therefore couldn't have been specifically targeted by, officers because of his race. To not explicitly address the possible workings of racism in the follow-up protest is to allow a color-blind discourse of social justice profit from the violence to which a Black body was subjected.

Perhaps the appropriate spot for the Black Lives Matter mural was right where Santos was arrested. Maybe the next time protestors return to the airport they'll manage to gain entry to the premises and paint the mural on the runway. Only this time, the intent would not be for visitors to look out the window and feel welcomed here, but for them to reconsider their vacation and book a return flight upon landing. Maybe the most faithful translation of Black Lives Matter is *Nuestras vidas antes que sus ganancias*. But those lives must be understood to be Black. And in Puerto Rico you simply can't take such an understanding for granted, so it must be spelled out: *Nuestras vidas negras antes que sus ganancias*.

Blackness functions as an erasure in Puerto Rico (Godreau 2015). By this, in part, I mean, that blackness is often stricken off, kept out, erased from the historical and contemporary sociopolitical and cultural inventories. But, also, that when it is finally and often forcefully made to appear, highlighted even, it does so in a type of social vacuum, the larger context receding from view. Santos's arrest cannot be seen as racially motivated, because—it appears— the protest would risk becoming about race and racism as opposed to about workers' concerns regarding the steady influx of tourists from the north during the lockdown. So often forgotten when broaching the pressing issues of the moment, race—and blackness, in particular—bears the threat of making us forget about the "real" issues at hand. It doesn't matter that Santos's arrest— visually—was much more reminiscent, on account of the violence carried out by the many white arms pushing and pulling down on his Black body, of the brutal and fatal arrest of George Floyd. Santos is only visible as a labor leader. He is not allowed to appear as a Black man. We can see the violence, but we are unable—or unwilling—to publicly, explicitly, name the type of violence it is and the type of person that this violence is designed for.

The charges against Santos—misdemeanor assault against a police officer and obstruction of justice—were eventually dropped as part of an agreement between prosecutors and the defendant's lawyers. In exchange, Santos vowed to not file a civil suit or administrative complaint against the officers involved in his arrest. Police, according to the news report, "are more wary of getting sued than they are of not infringing upon people's civil rights." Police, it seems, are also weary of the potential for protests to erupt anywhere, at any time:

> The parking lot [adjacent to the court building] was filled with officers, special operations vehicles outside and inside the court building it was swarming with officers. Some visitors admitted to never having seen such a high display of police presence in the court, not even in cases involving drug traffickers. (Cotto 2020; my translation)

The brief newspaper note makes no mention of the role race may have played in both the initial arrest and the subsequent show of force at the courthouse. The omission, while not surprising, is significant, considering that the only formal news outlet that covered the court proceedings—and thus, the one I am referencing here—is Puerto Rico's longest running and most heralded leftist periodical. Hence, the critical commentary on police officer's disregard for civil rights. The lack of engagement with the "small matter" of race has at least one important, and pernicious, effect: it subsumes Santos's experience as a Black man assaulted by police under the narrative of historical abuses committed by officers against radicals. As such, what happened to Santos could have happened to anybody else there. And anybody else, regardless of skin color, would have brought out police on parade for their day in court.

And so, what to do with Santos's arrest? How do we go about engaging a critical race perspective in our consideration of events, where the role of race seems, at best, secondary and messy, and at worst, irrelevant? To be honest, given the police's horrid treatment of protesters and political dissidents here (American Civil Liberties Union 2012), it is very likely that anybody else— regardless of color—could have been treated the same as Santos, or worse. Perhaps the way to engage a critical race perspective here is to ask how likely are white protesters to be treated by police in that manner outside of scenes of political confrontation? Does the vulnerability they come to inhabit as protesters carry over to other locations and contexts? The scant statistical evidence available would seem to suggest that whiteness or light skin in Puerto Rico is afforded some level of protection against unlawful and/or violent police intervention. According to police watchdog group Kilómetro Cero (2022), the islanders who report the highest levels of police intervention live in predominantly Black or racially diverse neighborhoods. One could thus make the argument that Santos, as a Black man, did not have to resort to public acts of protests to find himself in a precarious position at the hands of police, whereas whatever number of white or light-skinned bodies were present on the street that day only *became* vulnerable to the extent they took up space on the street as a method of dissent. The moment those bodies were made to return to the places, spaces, and contexts of their everyday life they ceased to be at risk, while Santos's body never really exits the site of possible police confrontation and repression.

Incidents like Santos's arrest remind us that the sense of "we" that undergirds even our most urgent and radical movements for liberation glosses over the heightened precarity of *some* of the dissenting and precarious bodies that assemble under the banner *nuestras vidas antes que sus ganancias*. It is a "we" that, though useful and important, and ultimately hopeful, can very well come at a cost, if it is assumed uncritically. Specifically, it comes at the cost of that Black body held down by white or lighter skinned hands. A body that must be publicly recognized as Black in order to identify the violence it is subjected to. The continued refusal to do so is also a sort of profiting. It too is an illegitimate taking.

17

For Life

On the forty-fifth day of the state-ordered lockdown due to the Covid-19 pandemic, a protest, under the moniker *Caravana por la vida* (Caravan for Life), took place in the financial hub of San Juan, denouncing the governor's refusal to open school cafeterias to feed the hungry. The organizer, Giovanni Roberto, a Black 37year-old man, was arrested by state police officers who—contrary to protesters—were breaking protocol as it pertains to the use of facemasks. Roberto was held in custody for ten hours. He was released that night as a judge found no basis for the obstruction charge put forth by prosecutors (Redacción 2020). His unlawful arrest pointed to what has become a staple of Puerto Rican public policy: the increasing repression and corresponding criminalization of the Black, the poor, and the oppositional members of Puerto Rican society (LeBrón 2019).

In February 2011, Giovanni Roberto, then a student at the University of Puerto Rico (UPR), addressed a group of young Black men from the municipality of Loíza who had been hired by a private security firm to police the university campus. The night before, the young men had clashed with student strikers, who were occupying the campus in response to the implementation of austerity measures within and beyond the UPR. Roberto, speaking to the crowd gathered in front of the university gates, attempted to connect the stated motivations and concerns of student activists—accessible, quality education for all islanders—with the lived reality of young men hired by the security firm. He spoke:

> Part of my personal history and why I'm so convinced about what we're doing here is because I too come from a poor barrio, because I too am black like you. Because when I was little my parents couldn't find work,

like you can't find work now … I think we can all be equal and that we all have the right to be equal. Why is Loíza a Black township? Why is Carolina a Black township? Why are Dorado and Guaynabo considered *blanquito* townships? It's called racism, it's called institutionalized racism … They don't let us leave. Those born in Loíza, stay in Loíza. Those born in Carolina, stay in Carolina. And when we come here to fight every day is so you too can have an opportunity to break that cycle … .do you really think that this is the alternative that the government should offer to young people—that they arm themselves with sticks to attack other young people? I think that even though you're on that side today, tomorrow you should be on the other side. In the end, what we want is that you have the opportunity to study here. (my translation)

Not only was this a singular and transcendental moment within the context of the student strike—activists' discourse while explicit in its careful and critical consideration of the intersections of class, gender, and sexual orientation, lacked even the most cursory engagement with race and racism—Roberto's address stands out even today for its direct, willful and uncompromising denouncement of racism as a defining structural force in Puerto Rico. According to the activist, it's not that the firm hired poor young men, it hired Black men. It's not that it held an open call for solicitors, it's that it specifically recruited young Black men from Loíza—a coastal municipality with a considerable Black population that has been subjected to police repression, displacement, and disenfranchisement. It's not that Loíza is somehow unique in its social conditions and its location in the collective imagination, it is that both of these are a product of a larger system—structural and ideological—that differentially assigns resources and value to specific places and the people who inhabit them. It's not that Roberto, by virtue of becoming a university student, transitions into something different from the kids hired to beat him with a stick. It's not like this is news to young men and thus Roberto must enlighten them. It's that the space must be taken to address it plainly and publicly at the risk of forcing a break with the student discourse, and at the risk of the surrounding context being just too much for a connection to be made between the two opposing sides.

Marisol LeBrón, in *Policing Life and Death*, includes insightful fragments of her conversation with Roberto about this event:

According to Roberto, "the fact that part of the movement were white boys" who hadn't "lived the life that young Black, mostly male, people live" created an inability for many within the student movement to identify with the young guards and caused them to instead react with contempt. He continued, "So when they saw Black people, the way they were dressing, the way they were acting and talking, I felt a lot of people were rejecting them in a negative way. I heard comments and I felt bad. I felt angry. I'm part of a movement that does not understand this situation. The situation that causes those young people to be scapegoats, in a way. Or be divided against other young people." (2019: 161)

Here, again, two distinct and socially incongruous groups coincide on the same vision of blackness. On the one hand, there's the university administration, which, in its attempts to quell dissent and implement policies that would severely curtail the school's accessibility, brings the type of kids it does not cater to—because of race and class and geography—to do their worst on the kids presumably fighting for everybody's right to higher education. On the other, are the student strikers, who are unable—or unwilling—to see their counterparts as the future students of the open, accessible university they are ostensibly fighting to bring forth. The *ugly Black* is the point where the two political rivals meet; where their conflicting visions of what is best for Puerto Rican society find common ground. This, then, is how strikers and administrators both serve whiteness. What Roberto attempts to do here is to make that common ground the principal site of contention. He thus makes a racialized map of the island, defining some municipalities as white, others as Black, and stressing how Black spaces are designed not to serve as homes but as prisons: "Those born in Loíza, stay in Loíza. Those born in Carolina, stay in Carolina."

Roberto's is a double call: a reprimand and a call to generosity. The reprimand is for the "white boy" student strikers, to live up to the radical principles of their discourse: they do not get to decide what type of student is agreeable to their goal of an open university; they must commit to their call for openness even if their whiteness has corrupted their vision so much that they cannot see the young Black men at the gates as desired fellow students. The call to generosity is to the young men in the security detail: Roberto calls on them to support a movement that excludes them. They are, in a way, being asked to act as if the call of the student strikers for a more accessible university was directed at them too. In this sense, it is not a call to join the student movement. But a call to forgive. To forgive the students for their white privilege. Even if what they deserve is to be hit upside the head with a stick. And maybe they do deserve it. But, if so, it must not be at the university administration's bidding; it must not be in the service of whiteness.

A student striker, I listened to Giovanni's speech at the gates. Not only was I one of the *blanquitos* he was referring to, but I was also born and raised in one of those white towns where Loíza was talked about as if it were another country. I'm trying to remember how I reacted to the security guards hired by the administration, if the outrage and disgust I remember feeling were somehow race-related. I remember how in the spring prior to Giovanni's speech, in the first part of that strike, during which the students occupied the campus for sixty-two days, we had countless discussions on issues of class and gender and sexuality, and how these markers affect student life. I don't remember a single conversation about race. It only came up months later when the kids from Loíza showed up. And even then, it didn't really come up until Giovanni spoke at the gate. What came up was the fact that these "thugs" had been given license to run amok inside the campus. What came up was the students had been deliberately put in danger. What came up was that young men who had no business being in school were now running things in the school. Which is how race usually comes up in Puerto Rico: in code, in context, out in the open but seldom openly.

Regarding both context and code, the law students' camp, where I was in during the occupation, was called Beverly Hills. Natural Sciences was called Disney. Social Sciences was Sparta. The Beverly Hills moniker, in part, responded to the perception—accurate or not—that the average law student came from a more privileged socioeconomic background than the rest. But importantly, it also responded to the perception—100 percent accurate— that law students' scope of protest actions was more limited than that of our counterparts. We Beverly Hills kids were all for sit-ins and other instances of peaceful resistance but tended to balk at direct confrontations with police. "Beverly Hills" then was code, in this context, for both well off and put off by our fellow strikers. In this sense, it very much summarized the overall *blanquito* condition: we were a part of the larger group, but our deep-seated beliefs and values were routinely offended by what we perceived as wayward or violent or irresponsible. Thus, there was this pervasive sense amongst our group that it was up to us to "save face" for the student strikers with the media, which tended to gravitate more heavily toward our camp. As a result, the story told from the inside of occupied student campus was mostly the story told by the group of students most unlike the rest. The logic was that law students, because of their academic formation, were the best suited to speak of the intricacies of legality, politics, and protest. In essence, we knew the law. But, also, we looked and sounded like the sort of university students the mass public would take seriously: clean-shaven, well-spoken, and peacefully resisting. Now that I think of it, several of the striking law students came from the white towns Roberto called out in his speech. And none, that I can remember at least, came from Loíza.

A few days after the Caravan for Life, video and photos surfaced on social media of a caravan of a different sort: members of an incoming senior class at one of the most exclusive private, catholic schools in one the most exclusive neighborhoods of San Juan broke the lockdown and all manner of social distancing protocols by driving from a public plaza to the beach where they hugged and mingled and posed for pictures (Metro Puerto Rico 2020). Even though there is a mobile precinct in the plaza where they first assembled, no police intervened at any point during their outing. Social media users critical of this event and of the lack of police intervention were quick to draw comparisons between the Caravan for Life and the caravan of *blanquitos*. The former was deemed an unlawful gathering and a threat to public health, while the latter was allowed to take place without even the most minimal police intervention or surveillance, as if for that very select group of kids in that time and place, there was no lockdown, no fear of contagion.

This event marks, for me, the quintessential element of *blanquito* as an identity and a social dynamic in Puerto Rico: *blanquitos* get away with things. It's not so much that *blanquitos*, individually and as a group, can afford to be daring or oblivious in a bankrupt island colony during the Covid-19 pandemic, but that the bankrupt island colony's government will willingly absorb the cost of their obliviousness or their daring. Roberto, we were told, had to be arrested because his actions put people at risk of infection. These kids weren't even rounded up and escorted home.

I would like to pause here briefly in the image of a round-up. After Casellas's arrest, Black or Black-looking kids from a neighboring community were *rounded up* and brought into a police precinct for questioning. During the student strike, Black or Black-looking kids from Loíza were *rounded up*, promised payment, and driven to the UPR to strike fear into the hearts of student strikers. In contrast, while the island was in lockdown, elite white kids were allowed to roam free on public property in a manner similar to, say, how the kids from the Jesuit school were allowed to get on with their lives after allegedly committing federal fraud while a public-school student was arrested in a bank terminal.

If white privilege means anything around these parts, it is the ability to evade the multiple ways in which islanders can be *rounded up*, lumped together, under the most dubious or downright nefarious considerations and get thrown into a something or be kept out of something. Following Roberto, "If you are born in Carolina, you stay in Carolina. If you are born in Loíza, you stay in Loíza." But if you are born in Guaynabo, or you are born in Dorado, or you are born in Condado, the world—or at least the select parts of the island that most resemble the most desirable parts of the world—is yours. This white or whitened world can, depending on the situation, encompass beaches and plazas, which are public. It can encompass the UPR, which is public too. It can even extend to the sites and sounds of opposition, where everybody is meant to be free so long as they look and talk and act like us good Beverly Hill kids.

18

Translation at a Loss

In 2013, former secretary of state and pro-statehood lobbyist Kenneth McClintock announced on social media his decision to follow in the footsteps of one of the luminaries of the African American activist tradition and protest what he believed where unjust regulations that negatively affected Puerto Ricans as a whole. He wrote on his public Facebook profile:

> Those of us who travel frequently and believe in equality should protest those Airlines that, now allowed by the FAA to do so, are nct allowing Personal electronic Devices (PED) to remain on from gate to gate throughout the flight. Several airlines have adopted the new rules for all their flights, except to—and from Puerto Rico and the U.S. Virgin Islands.
>
> Next time that I go on vacation I have decided that I will observe the US rule and inform the flight attendant that I will not heed the airline's instruction to turn off the allowed PEDs simply because it's a flight departing from San Juan.
>
> If they remove me from the plane, I will allow them to remove me peacefully.
>
> If they want to process me, so be it.
>
> Rosa Parks did it and the discriminating rule she did not obey was changed.

I'm pretty sure nothing came out of this statement; that is, there were no public reports of McClintock making good on his promise and staging some sort of peaceful protest in a commercial flight. Perhaps the regulation was changed soon after. Or maybe he benefitted from airplane personnel's lack of enforcement. In any case, what interests me here is not the former secretary's political integrity so much as to consider exactly how Rosa Parks comes to matter, for McClintock. Specifically, I'm curious as to what, from the former secretary of state's perspective, did Rosa Parks "do" and what she—as an African

American radical—might mean to him as a white Puerto Rican statesman. But first, another anecdote.

In 2018, Juan Taylor, a young Afro Puerto Rican man from the diaspora, traveling from Puerto Rico to New York, uploaded a (since deleted) video on *Youtube*, where he documented a fellow passenger's refusal to sit next to him due to his skin color (Giovanetti 2016). The passenger is heard in the video yelling to the flight attendant that she will not sit next to *el negro ese* (that Black man). Taylor's travel companion is also heard explaining to him that she was calling him a "n*****." The video went viral and was covered by several news outlets in Puerto Rico. Criticism of the woman's attitude and actions was so widespread and vicious that Taylor felt compelled to intervene on her behalf. Critics particularly made fun of how the woman rejected being labeled a racist, seeing as she was *trigueñita* (wheat colored). Thus, the incident became notorious not so much because of the virulence of the racist sentiment displayed by a passenger who refused to sit next to a Black man, but because the woman—depending on onlookers' perspective—was herself (kind of) Black.

It's easy, I think, to see Rosa Parks here. When Taylor's travel companion warns him that the complaining passenger has just called him a "n*****," he is skillfully navigating through the complex interworking of American and Puerto Rican racist systems. As discussed, there is no Spanish equivalent for the racist epithet, but context can dictate how the Spanish word for Black can be deployed and/or understood as a racist assault. In this case, given that *negro* is offered as a reason for the woman's refusal to occupy her assigned seat next to Taylor, the word—much like *negrito* was used by Casellas in his racial hoax— does come to mean "n*****." As such, the translation is linguistically incorrect but politically accurate. It makes the racist logic of the woman's refusal explicit. While the woman, for all intents and purposes, had been clear in telling her fellow passengers and flight attendants why she would not sit next to Taylor, it is Taylor's flight mate that connects her personal prejudice to systemic racism; his mistranslation gives the incident meaning in a fashion similar to Parks when she refused to give up her seat in a segregated bus.

McClintock on the other hand is merely poaching. He plucks Parks as a historical referent from her context and capriciously ties her to his cause. In his call to action, he vows to follow Parks' example of righteous civil disobedience, but really, he is merely dressing up an individual complaint against a regulation—which, however discriminatory it may be, it certainly would not and should not be at the forefront in the struggles against US colonialism. Furthermore, the reduction of what Rosa Parks did to a simple question of transgressing an unjust regulation—without any further consideration as to the question of white supremacy—is ludicrous and offensive. One might ask of McClintock, for example, who specifically is he thinking of when speaking on behalf of "those of us who travel frequently and believe in equality"? I wonder if, and how, Taylor might figure in this collective McClintock is referencing.

It might seem like I am being harsh—and ultimately unfair—in my reading of the former secretary's proclamation, but McClintock's use of Parks here is symptomatic or a larger trend among members of his party and of pro-statehood islanders in general: the willingness to connect the plight of Puerto Rico as a colony of the United States with the struggle for civil rights of African Americans. Now, to be clear, there is of course common ground to be found in the careful consideration of the historical, ideological, and economic foundations of US imperialism in Puerto Rico and the US racial state regarding African Americans. The issue is that McClintock and his fellow party members comfortably sidestep the question of race and racism when making these comparisons and completely ignore the matter of racism among Puerto Ricans. Parks and Martin Luther King Jr., for example, are often quoted because their speeches and writings contain the buzzwords statehooders treasure: equality, first-class citizenship, and the call for America to live up to its promise. As such, civil rights luminaries and the African American population are just rhetorical resources with which (white) statehooders can articulate their claim. This becomes further complicated when one considers that not only does the pro-statehood party ignore matters of racism in Puerto Rico in their public policy proposals and party platform, but several of their top figures readily conform—in terms of demography, aesthetics, and politics—to the *blanquito* imaginary and are responsible for one the most discriminatory and violent public policies in recent history.

In this sense, Rosa Parks would only be even remotely applicable to McClintock by the most self-serving—and contextless—of analogies. Her name, image, and activism thus arise during the careful drafting of a social media post as the politician is comfortably seated in his chair, free of harassment from both airline personnel and fellow passengers. In contrast, Rosa Parks appears in the Juan Taylor incident, insomuch as his flight mate must navigate a situation in which they have just been thrust: called "n*****," but not really, by a woman who—depending on who you ask—might also happen to be Black, but not really, and Puerto Rican, like him. Only she certainly does not read him as a fellow Puerto Rican. The logic being what made Taylor *negro* and therefore an unsuitable character for her to sit next to on a plane is his perceived foreignness. He is darker and English-speaking. As such, he might not register for her as a fellow *trigueñito* or *negrito* from Puerto Rico. He registers as a young Black male. There is no shared culture as buffer to mediate the encounter.

This is pure speculation, of course, but it is consistent with the prevailing view of blackness on the island, where those perceived to be "really" Black are instantly thought of as foreign (Arroyo 2002). They are taken for Dominican, or from the Virgin Islands, or from the US mainland, depending on the locale and context of the encounter, as well as other defining features (language, socioeconomic status, etc.). In Puerto Rico, blackness is folkloric, or its foreign, or its threatening. Consequently, people are invested in positioning themselves and (beloved) others somewhere in the middle. The middle then is filled with islanders who might not be readily defined as white or Black, more like *trigueño* or *café con leche* (coffee with milk) or *quemaíto* (lightly burnt), terms that on the surface might appear benign and even give the impression of the relative unimportance of race on the island, but that does the hard ideological work of separating Puerto Rican identity from blackness. Only most of us would never admit to this desire to separate. Afro Puerto Rican culture and people need to remain close enough to be claimed when it is convenient, but distant enough to not endanger our collective vision of a whitened sense of self.

What's especially tragic about the Juan Taylor incident is that both he and his aggressor are the Venus. In the plane, he is perceived as being in the woman's way. And then on the video, the woman is ridiculed for not realizing that she too could have made for a less than ideal flight companion. It does not matter whether she sees herself as *trigueñita* or Black. It depends on who's looking and who's judging. What matters is that she's darker than whoever might be assigned a seat next to her. And in Puerto Rico, fake fingernails can make you darker. Rollers in your hair can make you darker. Holding two gas cans in line at a gas station in the wake of a natural disaster can make you darker. As can being on food stamps. Or living in public housing. Or having lost one or more of your high school classmates or neighbors to street violence. Or having only set foot in a resort to report to work in the resort. Or being one of the handful of Black students in a high school class. Or being the son of a famous professional wrestler as opposed to the son a renowned lawyer or doctor or architect. Your anger or your distaste or your moral judgment, on the other hand, can—and will—make you white. Or, white enough to pass. However briefly.

19

Ransacked

In Vanessa Vilches's short story *Medir el territorio* (To measure the territory) from her collection *Geografías de lo Perdido* (Geographies of the Lost) (2018), the protagonist, Cecilia Martínez, a young geographer who works as a tour guide serving white American and European tourists, is sitting on the beach with her friends enjoying a weekend getaway. They spot a large group of tourists in catamarans near the coral. She complains about them wrecking the environment (and in unstated way, of wrecking her day, her country, the little life that is to be had here by people like her and her friends, in a place where a young woman with a geography degree is useful insofar as she can remember to smile and act as if visitors are really interested in whatever she has to say while on tour). Her male friend, Tito, responds to her complaint:

> Wow, what a hater, Ceci, Tito said. They come here to have a good time, like us. They have the same right to, no? Plus, as you well know, they pay quite a bit to be here. Yeah, right, Ms. Ecology. Like you're one to talk. (Vilches 2018: 29; my translation)

It is a reprimand, meant to invalidate her denouncement on account of his friend's perceived complicity with the rowdy visitors. She, after all, makes her living on tourism. Which is to say, her life—as she knows it, including a nice weekend escape to the beach with her friends—is possible thanks to the unruly visitors. In this sense, she is not so much complicit as caught. Or stuck. In Vilches's terms, at that moment—at all moments—Cecilia feels "invaded," "ransacked." But to voice such a sentiment to others—even those closest to you—is to risk being called out on one's lack of political purity. The question becomes what could she do to make a living in the colony that would allow her to voice her complaint without being made to shoulder some of the blame for the sociopolitical conditions of the place she inhabits. Or, rather, all the blame, as the tourists remain at a safe distance from the site of the exchange between Cecilia and her friend. They are oblivious to both her denouncement and his defense of them. Which, of course, makes the critique—no matter how accurate, articulate, and/or necessary—ineffective from the moment of its enunciation. And, therefore, it makes Tito's defense useless, pathetic. Tourists, we know, will continue to arrive in droves here regardless of how the Titos and Cecilias of this corner of the world feel about it. In this sense, it is hard, as a reader, to not feel sadness for both characters. You, of course, empathize with the protagonist, who, perhaps, when given the choice between waiting tables in a restaurant, opted to put her studies to use by offering some perspective on the place she inhabits to a group of people who are not looking for perspective. And you also empathize with the friend who calls her out because if there is anything worse than your political opposition failing to register for your stated oppressors, it is your willing acquiescence to the oppression also going unnoticed.

There is no mention of race in Vilches's short story. The tourists are simply American. Cecilia is simply Cecilia. Because they're American one presumes them to be white. Because Cecilia is, well, a Puerto Rican college graduate, who, we are told, completed all or some of her studies in Spain, one presumes her to be white. Or at least not Black. But there is nothing in the text that demands that reading. By the same token, that Cecilia references belonging to a family of Puerto Rican nationalists, or nationalist sympathizers; that her grandfather owned a small grocery store where he offered pro-independence fighters refuge; that though she studied abroad, she did not attend university in the United States; that upon finishing her degree, she is back in the place of her birth, struggling to get by as a tour guide, as opposed to, say, working for some well-to-do or well-connected family member, implies that while Cecilia can be imagined to be white, she most certainly is not a *blanquita*. And because she is not a *blanquita*, it is completely possible that—depending on the reader—she may be envisioned as darker skinned, even Black. The same goes for her friend Tito. The local imaginary allows for this. Moreover, it allows for Cecilia to be imagined as light or as dark as every and any individual reader desires, and for that variation to be understood to have no discernible effect on the plot. One could say it is a typical Puerto Rican short story.

I wonder, is this how fiction—even politically progressive, critical fiction like Vilches's story—saves us from blackness in Puerto Rico? Is this how a Puerto Rican character manages to always pass for white? Or is there political value in all possible readers being able to envision Cecilia—in the complexity and precarity of her position—as they see fit? Is the quality of feeling ransacked, caught in the colony the precise point where Puerto Ricans across the color spectrum can coincide, and can this sense of commonality prove generative for purposes of exploring race and racism in Puerto Rico in an open, critical— but not a fracturing—dialogue?

Such a dialogue does not take place in the story. The characters remain unraced, and instead of hearing his friend out, Tito shames her into silence: *Like you're one to talk.* It occurs to me, though, that Cecilia is the one to talk, as she is living—and struggling—with the contradictions of being against what she recognizes as an oppressive sociopolitical dynamic (in this case, colonialism), while at the same time directly working for it—and however marginally, profiting from it: if there were no American tourists around perhaps she would feel a little less ransacked, but if there were no American tourists around perhaps she would have a harder time making a life for herself. Cecilia, of course, is not alone on this. Tito, though the story does not offer this background information, is likely in a similar position. We can see in the story, however, how the precarity of his condition does not impede him from silencing his female friend. In this exchange, the author shows how gender impacts and complicates experiences of disenfranchisement. As readers, we are missing how race might further complicate the social dynamics among the two friends.

The point, however, would not be to label one of the two characters as privileged with regard to the other. In fact, I would propose that in Puerto Rican context, the discourse around precarity might be a better vehicle to engage critical discussion and reflection on race and racism than the discourse around white privilege. Because, as discussed, privilege outside of elite circles is so slight, the concept would seem alien to most of the population. And while this is to be expected when broaching racism in a purported racial democracy, it's possible that white privilege, as a concept, alienates more on account of it not aligning with how most people—regardless of color—live their life, than simply because it makes of color an issue. If such is the case, then from a strictly pedagogic and mobilizing perspective, it makes no sense to stress the idea of privilege among islanders, and instead explore and expand on the many dimensions of precarity once facts such as race are considered. If most of the population is seeing scarcity and struggle around them, they are perhaps more likely to consider further degrees or types of struggles, than to search for and recognize unjust privileges they may have on account of their race but that have failed to amount to a higher quality of life.

This is the reason why a slogan like *our lives before your profits* finds purchase within and beyond protest circles. It is also why, on the heels of Ricardo Santos's unlawful arrest, it should have been our Black lives before your profits. The heightened precarity of Black existence on the island becomes visible within the context of an already untenable situation for all workers. It is also why Cecilia must too be raced. Because her skin tone can very much affect, for purposes of the story and its impact on readers, her experience as a young geographer looking to make a life for herself in the Puerto Rico of today as a tour guide for white American and European tourists. If she were raced, the author would be forced to further tease out the particularities of her being ransacked. Which, again, most people here are. But the sense of commonality—for purposes of teaching and organizing—means nothing if most everybody presumes everybody else to be white, or at least not Black.

It is, however, a whiteness-in-context. While I have often interpreted the sort of self-identification that tends to "pop up" in surveys related to race and racism in Puerto Rico (see, e.g. Lloréns, García-Quijano, and Godreau 2017) where respondents describe themselves as *white but Puerto Rican* as obvious attempts to distinguish themselves culturally from white Americans, it occurs to me that there might be something more to that qualification. "White but Puerto Rican" could be generously interpreted as an individual recognition of race as arbiter of privilege and exclusion within a society. It's not simply that a respondent sees herself—or would like to see herself—as phenotypically white, but rather that she recognizes that there is *something to* whiteness. However, whiteness in Puerto Rico is conditioned by the sociopolitical and economic realities of the place, where the fact of being from here and having to live here limit the scope of protection and privilege that usually accompanies whiteness.

I know that this is an outrageous—and incredibly hopeful—claim. But the insistence on social context seems paramount to me when considering whiteness in Puerto Rico. Context may in fact be the most important word in the study of Puerto Rican racism today. While some may understandably argue that calls to contextualize island race constructs and dynamics have historically proven to be thinly veiled efforts to dismiss or explain away the gravity or extent of racial discrimination here (Mercado 2020), the public dialogue now—spurred by the present Black Lives Matter movement in the United States—should be careful not to simply translate concepts, constructs, and concerns. It's not that these are alien to the Puerto Rican landscape, nor does it mean that the American intellectual and activist tools would prove useless here. But they will prove less than useful in ascertaining the specificity of Puerto Rican racism, if both activists and academics fail to account for people's sincere investment in the myth of *mestizaje* and the sense of sameness it fosters among islanders.

That the image of a Puerto Rican racial democracy is a hoax does not imply that it has had no discernible, and deep-seated, social effects over time. Nor does it mean that its only important social effect has been to make racism in Puerto Rico less than visible, and therefore more difficult to identify and eradicate. The myth of *mestizaje* is not like religious doctrine, blindly passed down through generations, regardless of changing social, political, and cultural conditions. It is an ideology. As such it must continue to find the necessary fit and footing as the society changes over time (Fields and Fields 2014). In order for it to maintain relevance, it must not lose its explanatory power. The fact that it is still regularly used across all segments of the population in Puerto Rico means that islanders—on an individual and collective level—continue to be invested in it. A big part of this investment implies people's blindness or refusal to see how white privilege and anti-Black racism operate in Puerto Rico, yes. But this refusal to see is accompanied by an equally strong, and deep-seated, belief, that we are all—somehow—part of the same historical community. While this sense of belonging does not and cannot eradicate racism—seeing as it is premised on a racist structure—it does render certain key manifestations of racism—specifically racist violence against Afro Puerto Ricans—incompatible with who "we are as a people." And while this doesn't make Puerto Rican society any less racist than US society, it does impress upon us the need to think through and develop context-specific tools for critical antiracist academic and activist work. I want to push this point even further: a sense of belonging—even a fraudulent one—can and I believe has acted as a deterrent for racist violence and aggression. It has also until very recently made a social reckoning with race and racism almost impossible.

And so, again, a character like Cecilia—immersed in the political, ethical, and affective conundrums in which colonialism sticks islanders in—must be raced to showcase the specificities and intricacies of the colonialist project in Puerto Rico among differently raced bodies. As written, the reader does not know whether Tito is looking to silence and shame her by enforcing his gender privilege. Or if the call to silence is a call out of sorts, with Tito speaking from an oppressed class position (Tito as a nickname can be read as coming from more humble origins than the given name of the protagonist). Or if racial dynamics are mediating that exchange in any significant way. And if they are, then both characters would still be sitting on the beach together looking out at the American tourists, with one or both of them, perhaps, being able to make a claim to whiteness, but a Puerto Rican sort of whiteness, which—for whatever privileges it may afford the bearer—can do nothing to stop the tourists from acting however they want to act on Puerto Rican soil and waters.

20

On Audacity

On June 24, 2020, Afro Puerto Rican scholar Marissel Hernández-Romero published a short op ed piece in *Claridad*, Puerto Rico's oldest pro-independence periodical. The piece was written in response to a column by queer scholar Beatriz Llenín Figueroa, published in the same outlet a day before. Llenín Figueroa's piece is a personal call to antiracism from and for white people. In her response, Hernández Romero (2020) denounces her white counterpart's naiveté, her lack of self-awareness, and emphasizes the need for her to become a better ally to Afro Puerto Ricans. She writes,

> You have to know yourself to be privileged to dare compare the suffering and experiences of black people with your place as white woman on the island. In doing so you turned the black antiracist struggle into one that has to do with the guiltiness and pain of a white person. (my translation)

At no point in the original article does Llenín compare her suffering to that of Black people. Nor is her text about the guiltiness and pain of white people. It is about the ethical and political obligation that white islanders have to act against racism. She writes, "I am not, nor do I pretend to be protagonist of any history, though I recognize that my skin, without recourse, is read ... as white" (Llenín Figueroa 2020; my translation). But it is this articulation of her whiteness as a sort of imposition—and at another point in the article as a "random" occurrence—that bothers Romero, as she understands it to be an attempt to avoid personal accountability for her white privilege. Romero writes, "What does white at random mean? Are you suggesting you have no responsibility to eradicate the inequalities that black people face in this country because you did not choose to be white?" (my translation) The issue is complicated further by Llenín's references in the article, as they are pulled not from the local Afro Puerto Rican intellectual tradition, but from neighboring Caribbean nations and African American scholarship. Romero thus questions her white counterpart's commitment to antiracist struggle in Puerto Rico seeing as she either is not familiar with, or does not care for, local Black theorists. Finally, Romero blasts Llenín for claiming to be "antiwhite," when she should very well be aware of the vacuous character of such statements, when uttered by a white person. Romero writes:

> Thanks to your whiteness, you will suffer no consequence in your professional life, nor will your life be threatened for being anti-white. Nobody will question that affirmation, much less will they accuse you of being prejudiced against white people. On the contrary, they applaud your poetic, pretty writing … Can you imagine what would happen if I, a black queer woman, would dare to say that I am anti-white in Puerto Rico. I'm 100% sure that only daring to respond to you many of your loved ones will be mad at me. (my translation)

Now, one could reasonably argue that Llenín is at fault for not referencing local Black theorists and authors. One could reasonably argue that such a slight in a text meant to explore white islanders' role in antiracist struggle serves, as Hernández Romero points out, to further marginalize Afro Puerto Rican intellectual production. One could even say that her demonstrated preference for English-speaking Black theorists and thinkers—which she must translate to Spanish in her article—would seem to indicate that in attending to the specificities of racism in Puerto Rico, the white islander is "forced" to use her academic/cultural privilege to import and apply Black thinking from elsewhere to a place she considers bereft of the appropriate Black representatives of such a tradition. All these critiques, I think, would be fair. Perhaps even warranted. But what Hernández Romero—insomuch as she blatantly misreads and twists Llenín's analysis and engages in an interpretative practice oriented toward quick denouncement rather than understanding— exposes here are not ethical, intellectual, or political gaps in her interlocutor's thought process. What she is critiquing, I think, is Llenín's daring. What she finds fault in is the fact that Llenín dared to publicly foster discussion about the role of white Puerto Ricans in antiracism, speaking of course from the perspective of a white Puerto Rican woman. And that, in so doing, Llenín crossed the invisible line between the role of white ally and white usurper of Black struggle by declaring herself to be antiwhite.

In reading these two pieces, a question turns urgent: if white people can't be antiwhite then what is the point of antiracist struggle? That such a formulation may make the speaker and any possible interlocutors feel awkward or conflicted; that it may very well require a specific action plan to be drafted for such an affirmation to garner political effectivity does not make it an individual conceit or mere rhetorical device. The expression perhaps can be considered as a placeholder for a way of relating that is yet to come. Granted, this may make such an utterance, depending on the context, seem hardly more serious than wishful thinking. But is this not the type of wishful thinking we would like to foster? Moreover, would it not be more strategic to hold people accountable to the public manifestations of their wish-making, than discarding both dream and dreamer for presumed hypocrisy?

Lynne Segal speaks to this point urging us "to be a little less frightened of and more enthusiastic about our most scandalous desires and actions" (2017: 158). Exactly what is the danger of taking Llenín at her word? What is the harm brought upon antiracism and Black mobilization by allowing a white person the space to publicly reflect on and figure out her place as an actor on behalf of liberation? While white co-optation of Black intellectual production is real and widespread, and while it most certainly should be one of the target areas of any antiracist project, such concerns should not, I think, dictate how expressions of white antiracists are received. If there is any space to be allowed to white people it's the space to become antiwhite. I understand that this could rightly be classified as another manifestation of white privilege, but I sincerely believe it is the one form of white privilege that is useful to end racist oppression.

Llenín clearly will never be able to comprehend the complexities of living in a white supremacist society as a Black person. She never claimed she could. She should never, as a white person, become a spokesperson for Black Puerto Ricans. She didn't attempt to do so. But she can and should explore, experiment with, and evaluate, with joy, whatever possibilities may exist for her to challenge whiteness as a white person. Furthermore, this potential plan for action should not be dictated by others. It needs to be claimed and owned by the white actor. If not, it will always seem like she is doing the work for the exclusive benefit of another, at their behest, and as such, it is a work she can—even while being earnestly engaged by it—keep as separate from her innermost self. Political theorist Jodi Dean (2019), in her critique of allyship, writes:

> Allyship is a matter of the self, of what the self acknowledges, of the individual who stands alone, and of this single individual taking on a struggle that properly belongs to another. It's as if struggles were possessions—artifacts that individuals take on, over and into themselves—all the while being urged to see these acquisitions as something to which they, as the ally, have no right. At the same time, exactly what the struggle is, what the politics is, remains opaque, unstated, and a matter of the individual's feeling, attitude, or comfort level (2019: 18).

This is how Hernández Romero reads Llenín's piece: as a taking. As if she took the cause of and call for the end of anti-Black racism for herself without first requesting the permission of a Black scholar. In this way the problem of whiteness in Puerto Rico is represented more by white antiracism than by anti-Black oppression itself. Thus, in reading the Hernández Romero's critique, like Dean suggests, one remains unsure exactly what the larger collective project is supposed to be regarding racism on the island. The only thing made clear in her piece is that antiracism is the exclusive property of Black islanders. Llenín, it appears, needed a sponsor.

While whiteness as a social force is about privilege and exclusion, whiteness as individual lived experience and personal identity is more messy, complex. As critics like Tim Lensmire (2017) suggest, white people cannot be reduced to simple containers of social privilege. To do so is to disregard the anxiety and ambivalence that individual whites feel regarding their relationship with people of color, with fellow whites and with themselves. As Jess Row (2019: 52) aptly notes, "Normalcy does not imply weightlessness." Whiteness, though hegemonic, is not monolithic. The mere fact that an individual has been raced as white, does not imply an absence of dissonance between that individual and their social context. Paisley Rekdal (2021) explains:

> Whiteness is itself a fraught identity that contains multitudes, paradoxes and inherent conflicts. It is, historically, an identity that's been phenomenally flexible and rigid in its application, even as it has been relentlessly policed by those from within. Whiteness, as much as any other racial category, has

been open to dispute even if it has not been widely subject to persecution; it has been tied to class, labor, political power, geography, and even sexual preference; it has been treated as something that might be earned through work, education and through intermarriage, and in that, whiteness is always framed by the gaze of the non-White. (121–2)

White identities, I would argue, can be even more fraught in places like Puerto Rico, where distinctions are not as clear, or where boundaries can be more shifting. That islanders, regardless of skin color, are supposed to belong to the same imagined community, share the same ethnic and culturally diverse provenance, implies that—however problematic—white Puerto Ricans can have an affective relationship with blackness. Moreover, it implies that blackness is somehow related to who they are. The encounter then with the historical reality of whiteness and blackness on the island makes them not simply conscious of injustices committed to another, distinct group of people. It makes them involved. Antiracist thought and action would do well to tap into these feelings, instead of pushing the weight of the system, its origins, orientations, and effects, onto any and every personal biography, simply because the person is privileged by the system. Such a weight is not only unbearable, but it also obscures the complexities and contradictions inherent to lived experience, which include how white people make sense of the workings of privilege in their lives. Furthermore, it makes the turn to antiracist practice unlikely.

However paradoxical this may seem, we must make room for individual whites to critically attend to matters of race privilege. I'm not referring here to actual physical or social space, as white people are not lacking for platforms from which to pontificate on whatever issue strikes their fancy. I'm talking about intellectual, theoretical, ethical, and political room in which to critically, creatively, and honestly consider how privilege does and does not manifest in their lives. To refuse to do so makes us blind to important differences among different groups of whites and reinforces this pernicious binary of the "good whites" that see race and the "bad whites" that remain oblivious to it. This false and pernicious binary, then, allows for another: the bad "good whites" who want to be excused of their complicity with the racist system because of what they see or who want to be celebrated for what they see, and the good

"good whites" who repeatedly confess to their willed and unwilled complicity with a racist system, know their place in the struggle against racism, and limit themselves to denouncing their own privilege and amplifying the voices of the people they unwillingly oppress.

Antiracism is not a hero-making venture. But neither should it become an everlasting purgatory for the privileged few who are invested in changing the conditions that make their life better at the expense of others. Thus, white antiracists, I think, would do well to "forget" themselves at times and engage joy. The joy, yes, in referring to yourself, publicly and out loud, as antiwhite, even as it is your white privilege that makes such an utterance possible, because ultimately you have chosen to put your body in line to reduce that harm brought on against Black bodies. It *must* be okay for you to forget yourself like this occasionally, so long as you never forget where to place your body to always be in the way of white supremacy.

I am reminded here of Chicana feminist critic and writer Cherrie Moraga's retelling her encounter with renowned African American playwright August Wilson. She writes in her famed collection *Loving in the War Years* (2000):

> But for the shared history of miscegenation, Pulitzer Prize-winning playwright August Wilson and I have little in common, at least at face value. He is a man, man of large stature. (He must be over 6–2; 200 lbs.) He is an African American, a heterosexual, born in the East. I am a short, half-breed Mexican woman (I won't note my weight), born and raised in the Southwest. I am a lesbian. And yet, sitting in the last row of the packed 500-seat Mcarter Theater at Princeton University, I cried and called him "brother" out loud. I cried as he said to an audience of theater professionals, overwhelmingly white, "I am a race man" and "The Black Power Movement … was the kiln in which I was fired." I cried out of hunger, out of solidarity, out of a longing for that once uncompromising cultural nationalism of the 60s and 70s that birthed a new nation of American Indian, Chicano, Asian American and Black artists. (152)

There is a naiveté in Moraga that in today's cultural climate, some twenty plus years removed from her encounter with Wilson, would likely be met with heavy skepticism. Critics could rightly point out and object to how Moraga, in her desire to connect with the famed playwright's Black male nationalism, eschews her status as a white-passing Chicana. They could go even further, noting that not only does Moraga forget to mention her white-passing privilege—the one she herself brilliantly exposed and analyzed in the essay "La Güera"—but it could be argued, she also attempts to disguise it under the auspices of a "half-breed"—unraced—Mexican identity. Moraga thus could easily be taken to task for choosing to highlight how the intersections of gender and sexual orientation disempower her vis-à-vis her Black male counterpart, while simultaneously ignoring how race and color benefit her. Viewed from this perspective, her calling out to Wilson as a "brother" in the struggle for racial justice might seem, if not hypocritical, convenient, romantic, superficial. She continues:

> Although I knew he wasn't thinking of me, guerrera and embattled, I knew I carried the same weapons (more crudely made than his) and the same armor (mine surely more penetrable in my colored womanhood, in my sexuality). I knew, whether he recognized me or not among the ranks, that I was a "sister" in that struggle against a prescription for American theater that erases the lives of everyone I call my "pueblo". (Moraga 2000: 153)

I want to say, however, that there is a generosity to Moraga's gesture. A generosity that springs forth from her seeming naïveté. And, of course, Moraga is anything but naïve when it comes to matters of race, gender, and liberation. Two important elements underscore her cry and call to Wilson. First, her unabashed enthusiasm in hearing her fellow playwright define himself as a race man is grounded in her own extensive experience within Chicana liberation struggles. She is thus speaking from a specific social and political location, that is not, at bottom, so different from Wilson's. Second, Moraga, operating from a social movement perspective, recognizes the limits of individual (and authorly) intent: "I knew, *whether he recognized me or not among the ranks*, that I was a 'sister'" (my emphasis). The question of who's included in a call is not for the caller to decide. Once the call is made, anybody can answer as a "brother" or "sister." They, then, must engage the continuous personal and collective reflection regarding the terms of their belonging, their role in the movement. But being included is always the respondent's prerogative.

It must be remembered that racism, as a system, is relentless. Racists seldom show restraint. Antiracists should be audacious. And their audacity cannot be contingent on their privilege or lack thereof. To be audacious does not mean to be arrogant. Nor does it entail the foregrounding of the white antiracist's experiences, beliefs, and feelings to the detriment of the larger struggle. To be audacious is not to boast or poach. It means speaking up and out, but never over people of color. It does, however, imply that the white antiracist can and will speak of their own accord and not simply when called upon by those they are an "ally" to. And while this might mean that more mistakes will be made, audacity is not anathema to accountability. Those who dare to speak or act out against acts and structures of oppression, from a privileged position, assume a greater responsibility than those that simply intervene when allowed to by members of the oppressed group. It's the difference, perhaps, between being willing to help out and being willful. Sara Ahmed (2011), in discussing the uses and meaning of the will and willful, writes, "Willfulness can be attributed to those who refuse a command, or who refuse to be commanded" (245). A willful white antiracist refuses two commands: first and foremost, the command of the social structure predicated on the oppression on nonwhite peoples, even if it is meant to be in their benefit. And second, the command within antiracist struggles and movements to limit their intervention to the confines of allyship and to thus ascribe to a much too modest program of liberatory thought, speech, and action. Ahmed continues, "A diagnosis of willfulness becomes a mode of stranger making" (248). The audacious white antiracist is a stranger to both the larger social milieu of whites that conform to their social expectations and to the antiracist communities—online or on the street—that preach restraint to white allies out of fear of excess.

White antiracism, like whiteness itself, is a creature of excess. It inevitably infringes upon those oppressed by white supremacy. This, I think, is a truth all antiracists must come to understand and, to an extent, make peace with. I, for one, will never be aware of *everything* my white privilege endangers and/or makes worse, of everything it takes from my Black compatriots. My gestures— however virtuous or bullheaded—will always engender the possibility for racist harm. My development as an antiracist, however, will depend on the generous—though generosity does not necessarily mean kind, friendly, or patient—sincerity of my Black compatriots.

And so, let us imagine: How different would have Hernández Romero's response to Llenín's claim to antiwhiteness been if the critic would have written out of generosity? The generosity, again, to take Llenín at her word and push her to outline and specify the principles and practices of her white antiwhiteness, which would have perhaps led to a follow-up piece from Llenín that could have garnered another response from Hernández Romero, thus opening a critical discussion on whiteness and racism in the pages of the island's oldest and only left-leaning periodical. Instead, the subject was dropped, Hernández Romero having successfully called out her white counterpart, much like Tito did to Cecilia in Vanessa Vilches's short story: Yeah, right. Ms. Antiracism. Like you're one to talk.

21

A Modest Proposal for White Antiracism in Puerto Rico

The Black Lives Matter mural is still on Ashford Avenue, but the paint hasn't been retouched, making it hard to clearly see the message. I am unsure if the one atop the Hiram Bithorn Municipal Stadium is still there. The questions they provoke, of course, still linger: how exactly do Black Lives Matter in Puerto Rico? Does it matter that the people who promoted this most visible of public interventions in defense of Black lives were two white Puerto Ricans? Does an explicit embrace of blackness foster a more critical engagement with whiteness and white privilege on the island? In a previous chapter, I argued on behalf of the generosity of the former mayor and famous rapper's gesture. Here, I would stretch that argument further by making the following unabashed, admittedly superlative claim: the Puerto Rican future we dream of—at least from an antiracist perspective—is most forcefully and beautifully embodied by Bad Bunny.

The 28-year-old rapper, who now enjoys international fame at a level perhaps no other island-born musician has ever experienced, continues to court controversy due to the apparent contradictions between his stated ethical and political beliefs and the artistic and media content he produces. Pundits, for example, harp on the artist's potentially pernicious influence on children and adolescents who marvel at the fame earned by a college dropout who has in the past sold school notebooks with his likeness and logo. Or they question his solidarity with women's rights while being the face of the notoriously antiwomen musical genres of rap, trap, and reggaetón. Or they chide him for being brutally critical of the Puerto Rican government and lawmakers, while directly profiting from the legal measures put in place to attract investment and entice the wealthy. This sort of controversy, at least to me, seems less intriguing than what the artist in his production and performance across a whole host of platforms and in a variety of formats makes possible as it pertains to a defense of one's individuality and idiosyncrasies while pledging allegiance to broader, collective struggles for social justice. Consider, for example, two of his performances as they relate to gender violence.

In the wake of Hall of Fame Basketball player Kobe Bryant's death in a helicopter crash in January 2020, Bad Bunny released a short tribute song on YouTube. The song contained a lyric referencing Bryant's five championship rings and exalted a sixth, his wedding ring. The lyric, at best, comes across as naïve: Bryant was accused of rape in 2004. He famously refuted the allegations in a press conference with his wife by his side, sporting a new million-dollar diamond ring. Upon his death, as tributes to Bryant and his teenage daughter (who was with him in the helicopter crash) were delivered from seemingly everywhere, more politically progressive sectors were urging for, at the very least, a critical consideration of Bryant's legacy, especially in the context of #MeToo. Bad Bunny, by releasing this song, seemed to side with the fanatics, with those who resisted taking their dead idol to task for the alleged assault.

Fast forward to February of that same year, when the rapper performed in NBC's The Tonight Show, in a long black skirt and T-shirt reading: "They killed Alexa, not a man with a skirt." The attire he chose—and the message on his shirt—were in reference to a Black trans woman that was brutally killed in Puerto Rico after a third party authored a viral trans phobic Facebook post targeting her. Thus, in a matter of weeks, the rapper went from publicly mourning and celebrating the life of an alleged rapist to defending the life and demanding justice for the death of a trans woman.

One possible reading of these interventions—as well as his participation in Condado's Black Lives Matter mural—is that this is white male privilege at work. Sure, he helps fund a Black Lives Matter mural, but what does that gesture amount to in comparison to the fame and fortune he has amassed practicing a Black diasporic musical form? Sure, he performed T-shirt solidarity with trans people while donning a skirt on national television, but where is his solidarity when it's time to hold his idols accountable? To press the matter further, how, one could ask, is Bad Bunny any different from Kenneth McClintock aboard that airplane claiming to be following Rosa Parks example? How are the artist's interventions and performances not takings?

The one saving grace I can identify here is that Bad Bunny appears to be sincerely committed to his elected affinities. Contrary to McClintock, who, in referencing Rosa Parks, reduces the complexity of both the figure and the movement (from civil rights to the purported injustice of aircraft regulations), Bad Bunny in his interventions enriches the interpretative and analytic terrain of the discourse surrounding gender constructs and gender violence: it might seem like a small act for a male singer to wear a skirt onstage, but Puerto Rican rap scene is historically male-centered and homophobic to a fault. Thus, to be one of the premiere representatives of that genre and don a skirt is significant within context. Similarly, to team up with a local politician for a Black Lives Matter mural can seem like a convenient, risk-free co-optation of a social movement, but such a public embrace of blackness and of the struggle for racial justice in a sociocultural context predicated on the invisibility of blackness is also significant.

I would argue that what distinguishes Bad Bunny as a public figure intent on embracing certain social causes is precisely his level of investment, and the absence of a cohesive, logical narrative to help makes sense of these affinities. Contrary to other celebrities, the rapper's concerns, interests, and preferences on a personal and sociopolitical level do not appear to be heavily curated. They thus make for an awkward fit: the diehard Kobe Bryant fan who is also a trans rights advocate. As a result, they read—and he reads—sincere.

Bad Bunny, I would argue, in his disparate, conflicting, whimsical, and seemingly naïve interventions, enacts a radical, hopeful template for anti-oppressive action from spaces of privilege. He just *happens* to be a fan of Kobe, while he *happens* to believe in trans rights. Or in Black Lives Matter. And while these separate realities might not cohere within ideological strains in the Left, the artist expresses each, willfully, openly, *as if* there was no contradiction. It's not that he simply likes what he likes. It's that he is purposefully and publicly stating preferences and establishing affinities that both push him as white cis-gender Puerto Rican man to affirm expected interests and values *and* insert himself in the struggle for liberation of Black, queer, female peoples.

You could say it's a politics of *delight*. Complex, contradictory, and, even, error-prone, but not without thought and certainly not lacking in commitment. He seems motivated not so much by the desire to be on the *right side of an issue*, but rather by a desire to remain true, to be faithful to his elective affinities.

What I find valuable here is not that contradictions should be embraced and accepted without question, but rather that engaging the political does not imply an immediate surrender of all those parts, affects, and interests that may not necessarily fit with, or may even be dramatically at odds with, the political principles of the cause or movement one champions.

To expand on this point let me bring poet and essayist Ross Gay, who, in his *Book of Delights*, writes:

> What constitutes pleasant, it's no secret, is informed by my large-ish, male, and cisgender body, a body that is also large-ish, male, cisgender, and not white. In other words, the pleasant, the delightful, are not universal. We all should understand this by now. (2019: 28–9)

Following Gay, one could argue that Bad Bunny's politics not only allow for, but openly embrace and celebrate, how his particularities—with regard to race, class, gender, sexual orientation, yes, but also personal likes, guilty pleasures, and such—*inform* the vision of the world he wants to bring into being. This is important, because the world we want is a world in which ultimately our body will be able to fit in too. And if it happens that such a body is white, that such a body has learned to move in awe of the bodies of controversial basketball stars, well, so be it. What matters is that such a body recognizes the right to fulfilling delightful embodiment for everyone.

22

To Resist and Rescind

It's the little things that throw them off. Or, rather, that make me seem fallen from the graces of privilege and that make chance, quotidian encounters awkward, troubling.

The way I'm dressed. Coming from a long line of attorneys, prosecutors, and judges, those of the same ilk would expect me to look like I just stepped out of a courtroom. But my attire, on most days, would imply leisure. Only, I'm not wearing the recognizable brands, nor do I have the requisite accessories on. Say, we run into each other at the mall on a weekend. The men of my age, race, and class usually sport light-colored Bermuda shorts with a matching polo shirt, maybe a Ralph Lauren cap and designer loafers, no socks. I, instead, dress on the weekend like I dress most every day: jeans, T-shirt, sneakers. Most of my T-shirts have the names and faces of pro-wrestlers. Most of my sneakers have song lyrics or verses scribbled in black, blue, or pink marker. Which is how I used to dress when I was in college—a time when, regardless of appearance, they would likely guess I was on the way to living up to the family name, my appearance unlikely to outweigh my promise. But twenty years later, I appear to them not-quite-right, unsettled perhaps. Thus, my appearance too is unsettling.

Consider, for example, the way I introduce my partner as my partner and not my wife—we are not legally married. And while that is far from a taboo in present-day Puerto Rican society, good Puerto Rican families are sticklers for tradition. And, if not, then romantic partners are commonly referred to as *novios* (boyfriend-girlfriend), which points toward eventual marriage. *Compañera* (partner) is a term laden with leftist political connotations. And *blanquitos*—outside of grade school or certain workspaces—aren't *compañeros*. They're friends, colleagues, and associates. I'd just as well call her my comrade.

Thus, they look at me, at her, at us, as if they think we're up to something. That "something" is usually understood as a flair for the eccentric, which, in their mind, serves to disguise professional failure, or personal drama. Maybe drugs. Or financial ruin. But I don't look junk sick. And my attire does not signal a precipitous fall from financial bliss. It's more indicative of never having met the professional expectations and standards of a member of my race and class. Which is a failure and a tragedy, of a sort.

That our son does not bear my name nor the name of my father or grandfather, which are my middle and first names, respectively. That I'm too old to not have been married before. Too old for our first born. That we three do not bear the requisite marks of a good Puerto Rican family, other than the marking that is my family name and the fact that they know, or know of, the well-known and well-regarded members of my family. That I bear a physical resemblance to them. That, therefore, our son must also bear some resemblance to his grandfather or uncles (he does not), who are usually brought into the conversation at this point. If I am asked about them, I politely plead ignorance as to how they're doing, where they're living, and so on. This always strikes my interlocutors as strange to the point of silence. At which point, we graciously say our goodbyes. But sometimes, to my dismay, the silence is broken by a question.

They know I write books, so they make some type of blanket statement about having read something I've written, or rather, they mention having read a review of something I wrote, which prompts the question: *have you written something else?* Chances are, they are not actually interested in reading anything, much less in hearing me talk about my writing. But they—in their most gracious and committed selves—feel like they should engage me—on my ever so peculiar terms—for the sake of my mother, father, uncles, assorted ancestors—because I am ultimately part of that good family that they know. And feigned interest is a small price to pay for the sake of complying with the obligations of social privilege. I, of course, answer in the most cursory and polite way. But as my partner is quick to point out at the end of the encounter, there is often a slight shift in my tone, indicative of an apparent desire, she says, to please, to not break some sort of protocol, to make myself—and therefore, our family—recognizable to them.

She's right. These people are, after all, my people. Which is to say, I was parented in a similar way. Ana Ramos-Zayas explains:

Interlocutors in the El Condado sample led virtually the same lives that their own parents and even grandparents had led; they attended the same schools and clubs, grew up in the same neighborhoods, had the same occupations, knew the same families, married people they knew since childhood, and had dense social networks. I have never seen a more perfect example of what classical sociology has called "social reproduction" than what I witnessed in El Condado. (2020: 30)

Perhaps it's that density that pulls me in. The fact that for all that I find off-putting about them, I can't help but feel a profound, irrevocable sense of belonging. That, for all that I feel at home in my body and in my life—built as it is in definite reproach to the vision, values, and behavioral patterns of my race and my class—the home they remind me of—the social location they, however briefly but effectively bring me back to—is gut-level, instinctual. My body falls into place among them, even as my heart, mind, and political commitments lie elsewhere. And so, my answers tend to be brief but not curt, and I, almost without thinking, recur to using terms or turns of phrase, to physical gestures, even, that are particular to these people, *my* people: A certain boyish grin, when standing, facing them, arms on each hip, like a Superhero, nodding enthusiastically, while smiling to ask, "So, what have you been up to?"

It is at this point that I catch myself. I notice how I'm nodding or standing. I correct my posture, pull back. And concentrate once again on my edges, which I may soften throughout the rest of the interaction, but I'm not actively looking to disguise. So, if the conversation continues, it becomes clear—if it wasn't before—that something is amiss: I do not live in the same type of neighborhood as them. I am not in touch with fellow classmates. They did not see me at so and so's wedding, because I wasn't there. Social reproduction in these select circles might be dense, but you can always escape it.

I feel that, even considering my desire to be ill fitting but not totally off-putting, something always feels broken up or messed with during these chance encounters. The social cues are given by them. They are dutifully received and understood by me, but my response, if not a totalizing rejection, casts serious doubts as to whether I remain a willing and trustworthy member of the class. These doubts, I like to think, are enough to render our encounter and our relations strange. This strangeness, in turn, disorients my interlocutors however briefly, forcing them— in my mind—to find their racial and class bearings elsewhere.

These are subtle, miniscule breaks with expectations, yes, and certainly insignificant on a larger scale. But they also represent important life choices. They mark me as having made a decision. They signal a willingness, or more precisely, a willfulness to break apart from a set of race and class expectations. They suggest a delight in *messing with* the set of codes, gestures, and exchange of pleasantries and understandings, which make up the grammar of everyday life for the privileged few. And while this, in and of itself, cannot neutralize the primary, involuntary ways in which privilege operates in my life, it does imply a reproach of that social order, which in turn marks me as different, or damaged, or suspect.

I stopped short of adding "incorrigible" or "forever lost" to the list, because while somebody can always break through the density of social reproduction, there is no escaping the forever latent possibility of return. "Race traitor" always struck me as an odd term, insomuch the really sticky and socially significant parts of privilege are the ones you have little if any capacity to betray: how the surrounding social world accommodates your whiteness, allowing you to go about your life, even if the way you have chosen to make your life marks a break with the type of life you were born into. It is impossible to betray this social fact, because it exceeds your field of agency. What we commonly refer to as race traitors are people who continually look to not fulfill the expectations others like them may have of them. They're not acts of treason so much, as unspoken, and unacknowledged, agreements between loved ones and strangers that you, unilaterally, rescind. The distinction is important, because a traitor, once exposed, becomes persona non grata. But one can spend years rescinding these agreements on a regular basis, and the moment one opts in— by way of a gesture, a change of dress, or career—you are brought back into the fold, as if you never left. White privilege means that you are never canceled or disqualified as a potential contracting partner. Privilege, in this regard, is forgiving. It is always willing to welcome you back in, happily.

Perhaps, this is what Black antiracists—in the United States, Puerto Rico, and elsewhere—are hinting at when they impress upon their white counterparts the importance of owning their privilege. If so, often, the signals get crossed, because what seems to be asked of whites and/or what whites understand they're being asked to do is recognize all instances, locations, and dynamics where they are ultimately and unequivocally privileged vis-à-vis their Black counterparts. This, to me, is a futile task. At worst, it requires whites to be prescient, always anticipating—no matter the issue or circumstance—the precise manner in which they are unable to take a stance on the matter apart from disqualifying themselves from the conversation after giving an account of their privilege. At best, it directs their attention to everything that is immutable about their social conditions, rather than to those instances where they willingly, willfully cause some form of disruption. Because while privilege will always be glad to have you back, you have to want it.

This, I think, is what the old couple at the store was most perplexed by. Nothing about me communicates a desire to be taken in, claimed as one of their own. I always will be, of course, as it pertains to those aspects where it matters the most: access to essential services, political representation, treatment by the state, and so on. But the willful refusal to set a limit, to not replicate the affective structures in raising our son, for example, matters too. The choice not to partake in the social rituals that correspond to people of my race and class, and that therefore imply a recognition, acceptance, and extension of the exclusionary, or otherwise discriminatory values, beliefs, and behavior patterns these rituals are meant to uphold and communicate intergenerationally matters. It is not that it simply serves to register an individual break with the density of the social network and its corresponding reproduction, but that such breakages are possible and can also be communicated, learned, and, therefore, reproduced over time. Which is to say, in more concrete terms, that my son likely will not learn the same discourses, bodily gestures, coded messages, and implicit understandings that I cannot fully forget, but that I have learned to deemphasize, at least, in my everyday life with the people closest to me. What he would have to unlearn—as it pertains to affective, intimate, internal life of privilege—would be dramatically less. So much of what makes me *me* would be foreign to who and what he will make himself to be. This, I submit to you, is an antiracist victory. And though small, can be copied, mimed, adapted, repeated time and again across households and relationships. For the better.

23

Sons of María

The problem of Puerto Rico in the twenty-first century is the small problem of whiteness: how do we conceptualize it in relation to the specificities of local history and culture? How do we attend to it in institutional and communal life? How do we identify, highlight, and explain its workings in relation to more readily identifiable forms of oppression? Where might we pick and choose our intellectual tools from? At what point do concepts and constructs from elsewhere—those from the United States in particular—stop being useful in aiding our critical thinking and become more like a blinding imperial imposition? How do we broach the issue of white privilege skillfully? What aspects—if any—of the traditional Puerto Rican imaginary might be of use? Or does attending effectively to the small problem of whiteness on the island imply a call to abandon all existing forms of thinking and feeling Puerto Rican?

The problem of Puerto Rico in the twenty-first century is everything but whiteness: economic crisis, austerity politics, access to essential services, unresolved political status, gender violence, increasing inequality, mass migration, street violence, disaster capitalism, governmental corruption, and the corresponding lack of faith in public institutions. And yet, whiteness underscores all of this, somehow. It's just difficult to explain, without contradicting oneself or turning to examples from elsewhere, which frequently lead to mistranslation and misunderstanding. And so, at the risk of misunderstanding, allow me to finish with this admittedly irresponsible proclamation.

The sons of María are all white. They may or may not have identified themselves as such in the US Census. They, when pressed, might recur to one of those "quaint," "fluid" racial identities to describe themselves. They might not even be able to pass for white in Condado or Guaynabo City. But María's sons are as white as a Black Lives Matter mural atop of the baseball stadium for visitors to look at from the plane, or on the street in Condado for tourists to step on. As white as state police officers illegally and forcefully arresting a Black protestor. As white as his fellow protestors failing to denounce the possible racist motivations behind the arrest. As white as having poor Black kids from Loíza guard the public university against (mostly white) student strikers. As white as keeping white and Black kids from a public housing complex off a waterfront plaza. As white as writing a book about whiteness in Puerto Rico, in English, to complain about the lack of a sensible, open, and sustained dialogue on the matter of race and racism in a place, where most of us—white or Black—speak Spanish. In a place, where *negrito* can mean both "love" and "ugly Black." In a place where while we all might celebrate ourselves as the historical product of racial mixing, a white woman with three Black children in public is curious, strange.

María, as imagined by Rinaldi, can only have white children. It doesn't matter how often and how well the story of *mestizaje* is told. It doesn't matter how many Black Lives Matter murals are put up across the island. María's sons will be white until Puerto Ricans start imagining themselves *otherwise* in political protest, public policy, and daily practice. In art and literature. In the pedagogy of the classroom and in the ritual and routine of everyday life. We need imaginative acts that, instead of denying or diminishing the influence of white privilege in Puerto Rico, allow individuals and collectivities to *mess* with the complicated, ambiguous, unstable, and/or fleeting character of white privilege here, and thus align white identities with an alternate set of principles. I am calling for an unsettling and unsteady imaginative practice that pulls from each person's social, political, and cultural affinities, with daring and respect for self and others, that would help inscribe egalitarianism in bodies and relationships.

I'm talking here, again, about choice. The choice to let oneself be guided by the generosity of the gesture, one's own and those of others. The choice to not only remain attentive to the ways in which one, as a white person, is privileged, but also attend to the quotidian work of, however temporarily, partially, and imperfectly, rescinding your privilege. The choice to speak publicly and unapologetically from that space, where one can attest to acting audaciously on behalf of racial justice. The choice to remain willing to fail in such endeavors and be held accountable by others. The choice to resist the urge to apologize for one's birth, oneself, one's body, because the willfulness required of a white antiracist is not compatible with the obligation to assume the moral burden of an oppressive system as if it were one's own doing.

I'm talking here about audacity, which, again, does not preclude accountability. Instead, it embraces it as a tender, as opposed to punitive, concept. There is a path that can be readily traversed between partial recognition and dutiful repair. The audacious white antiracist recognizes some of the aspects of racist dynamics at work around her, recognizes some of the ways she is privileged by them, chooses to respond to a call to action, and if she messes up, when she messes up, is willing, and prepared, to repair whatever harm she may have caused. But the mere possibility that she may cause harm to somebody is not what determines her role and her work as a white antiracist. The possibility that she might, however unsteadily, open a path to justice through her commitment to antiracist action is what motivates her. It's what makes her *herself*.

In this precise sense, white people, Puerto Rican or otherwise, make the best antiracists. Like Moraga, they have responded to a call that may or may not have been meant for them. They have opted to position themselves as sisters and brothers, even when those they desire so much to see as kin would never consider them as such. Like Llenín, they are so valiantly vulnerable that they are willing to be taken to account for their desires and dreams. And like Domenech, they recognize both the importance of personal experience when challenging racism and the risks of letting their personal experience determine their careful consideration and interpretation of larger social systems, patterns, and dynamics.

I am not describing a type of person so much as a standard to live up to; the answer to the question *what does racism demand of those who benefit from it?* It demands that we be aware, not wary. That we be crafty, not guilty. That we become valiant, and not made to feel like villains. That we remain responsive to, and responsible for, whoever might call on us to step up. That we step up, even when nobody has ever thought to call on us. That our intervention catches them by surprise. That in catching them by surprise, we surprise ourselves, time and again.

References

Adams, T. (2012), "The Joys of Autoethnography: Possibilities for Communication Research," *Qualitative Communication Research* 1 (2): 181–94.

Ahmed, S. (2006), *Queer Phenomenologies: Orientations, Objects, Others*, Durham: Duke University Press.

Ahmed, S. (2011), "Willful Parts: Problem Characters of the Problem of Character," *New Literary History* 42 (2): 231–53.

Ahmed, S. (2014), *Willful Subjects*, Durham: Duke University Press.

American Civil Liberties Union (2012), *Island of Impunity: Puerto Rico's Outlaw Police Force*. https://www.aclu.org/report/island-impunity-puerto-ricos-outlaw-police-force. Accessed on 15 January 2023.

Arroyo, J. (2002). "Espejito, Espejitto: Raza y Formación de Identidades Puertorriquenas en 'You Don't Look Like' de Javier Cardona," In *Saqueos*, edited by Dorian Lugo, Editorial noexiste.

Arroyo, J. (2014), "Por Qué Ferguson," *80grados*, 28 November. https://www.80grados.net/por-que-ferguson/. Accessed on 15 January 2023.

Clemente, R. (2017), "Not in Our Name: Rosa Clemente Challenges a Puerto Rican White Supremacist in Charlottesville," *Atlanta Black Star*, 21 August. https://atlantablackstar.com/2017/08/21/not-name-rosa-clemente-challenges-puerto-rican-white-supremacist-seen-charlottesville/. Accessed on 15 January 2023.

Cordero Mercado, D. (2021), "Dramático el Salto en la Percepción Multirracial en Puerto Rico en el Censo de 2020," *El Nuevo Día*, 12 August. https://www.elnuevodia.com/noticias/locales/notas/dramatico-salto-en-la-percepcion-multiracial-en-puerto-rico-en-el-censo-de-2020/. Accessed on 15 January 2023.

Costa, J. (2020), "Arrestan Manifestante a la Entrada del Aeropuerto LMM," *Noticel*, 25 July. https://www.noticel.com/video/20200725/arrestan-manifestante-en-la-entrada-del-aeropuerto-lmm/. Accessed on 15 January 2023.

Cotto, C. (2020), "La Odisea del Arresto de Ricardo Santos Ortiz," *Claridad*, 5 August.

Dean, J. (2019), *Comrade*, London: Verso Books.

Díaz Rolón, A. (2021), "Justicia Cierra Casos contra Estudiantes por Fraude al PUA," *El Vocero*, 16 March, https://www.elvocero.com/gobierno/justicia-cierra-casos-con

tra-estudiantes-por-fraude-al-pua/article_9a5595aa-8689-11eb-8960-3b1dd4a0d 8f8.html. Accessed on 15 January 2023.

Dinzey-Flores, Z. (2013), *Locked In, Locked Out: Gated Communities in a Puerto Rican City*, Philadelphia: University of Pennsylvania Press.

Domenech, R. (2013), "¿Y esos Nenes de Quién Son?: Algunos Comentarios sobre Racismo Cotidiano," *Revista Cruce*. http://revistacruce.com/new_revi sta/?q=y-esos-nenes-de-qui-n-son-algunos-comentarios-sobre-racismo-cotidi ano. Accessed on 15 January 2023.

Domonoske, C. (2017), "In Puerto Rico, Containers Full of Food Sit Undistributed at Ports," *NPR*, 28 September. https://www.npr.org/sections/ thetwo-way/2017/09/28/554297787/puerto-rico-relief-goods-sit-undistribu ted-at-ports. Accessed on 15 January 2023.

Duchesne, J. (2008), "Síndrome Guaynabo City," *Hotel Saturno*, 7 June. http://hotel saturno.blogspot.com/2008/06/sindrome-guaynabo-city.html. Accessed on 15 January 2023.

Feagin, J., H. Vera and P. Batur (1994), *White Racism: The Basics*, New York: Routledge.

Feagin, J., and H. Vera (2008), *Liberation Sociology*, Boulder: Paradigm Publishers.

Fields, K. E., and B. J. Fields (2014), *Racecraft: The Soul of Inequality in American Life*, London: Verso.

Figueroa-Martinez, L. (2007), "New Puerto Rican Theorizing on Race," Puerto Rican Studies Association Seventh Biennal Conference, Ithaca, NY, 6 October.

Franqui-Rivera, H. (2014), "Michael Brown and White Privilege among Puerto Ricans," *Latino Rebels*, 4 December. https://www.latinorebels.com/2014/12/04/ michael-brown-and-white-privilege-among-puerto-ricans/. Accessed on 15 January 2023.

Fusté, J. (2019), "Residente en la Blanquitud Boricua," *80grados*, 15 February. https://www.80grados.net/residente-en-la-blanquitud-bori cua/?fbclIwAR3ynPq3QgyjSIhEQzBKBCSmQKgdNq86SPjQWsdj2WNMNFRg EkxNu4xeZwE. Accessed on 15 January 2023.

Gallop, J. (2002), *Anecdotal Theory*, Durham: Duke University Press.

Gay, R. (2019), *The Book of Delights: Essays*, Chapel Hill: Algonquin Books.

Giovanetti, J. (2016), "Señalar el Racismo de lo Efímero y Cotidiano," *80grados*, 12 February. https://www.80grados.net/senalar-el-racismo-de-lo-efimero-y-cotidi ano/. Accessed on 15 January 2023.

Godreau Aubert, A. (2018), *Las Propias: Hacia una Pedagogía de las Endeudadas*, Cabo Rojo: Editora Educación Emergente.

Godreau, I. P. (2015), *Scripts of Blackness: Race, Cultural Nationalism, and U.S. Colonialism in Puerto Rico*, Urbana-Champaign: University of Illinois Press.

Hernández Romero, M. (2020), "Desde el Cariño: Una Respuesta para Beatriz Llenín Figueora," *Claridad*, 25 June.

Jackson, J. (2020), "'We Take Anti-racism Seriously': The Story Behind the BLM Murals in San Juan, PR," *Remezcla*, 22 June. https://remezcla.com/culture/black-lives-matter-murals-in-san-juan-puerto-rico/. Accessed on 15 January 2023.

Kilómetro Cero (2022), *Licencia para Matar: Muertes por Uso de Fuerza Policial en Puerto Rico, 2014–2020*. https://static1.squarespace.com/static/5af199815cfd796ad4930e20/t/6239175bcdd64a29b2f4b7d0/1647908706107/2InformeLicenciaParaMatar+%286%29.pdf. Accessed on 15 January 2023.

LeBrón, M. (2019), *Policing Life and Death: Race, Violence and Resistance in Puerto Rico*, Berkeley: University of California Press.

LeBrón, M. (2020), *Against Muerto Rico: Lessons from the Verano Boricua*, Cabo Rojo: Editora Educación Emergente.

Lensmire, T. (2017), *White Folks: Race and Identity in Rural America*, New York: Routledge.

Llenín Figueroa, B. (2020), "La Negritud es un Archipiélago," *Claridad*, 24 June.

Lloréns, H., García-Quijano, C. and I. P. Godreau (2017), "Racismo en Puerto Rico: Surveying Perceptions of Racism," *Centro Journal* 29 (3): 154–83.

Lúgaro, A. (2020), "Hablemos del privilegio blanco ..." *Facebook*. 3 June. https://www.facebook.com/alugaro/videos/692771468172634/. Accessed on 15 January 2023.

McIntosh, P. (1989), "White Privilege: Unpacking the Invisible Knapsack," *Peace and Freedom*, July/August. https://psychology.umbc.edu/files/2016/10/White-Privilege_McIntosh-1989.pdf. Accessed on 15 January 2023.

Mercado, M. (2020), "To My Fellow BoriBlancos: When We Say 'Down with White Power,' We also Mean Our White Power," *NACLA*, 2 October. https://nacla.org/puerto-rico-white-supremacy. Accessed on 15 January 2023.

Metro Puerto Rico (2020), "Seniors Invaden Playa en medio de Toque de Queda y sin Mantener Distanciamiento," *Metro*, 7 May. https://www.metro.pr/pr/noticias/2020/05/07/seniors-invaden-playa-medio-del-toque-queda-sin-mantener-distanciamiento.html. Accessed on 15 January 2023.

Moraga, C. (2000), *Loving in the War Years: Lo que Nunca Pasó por sus Labios*, Boston: South End Press.

Morrison, T. (1992), *Playing in the Dark: Whiteness and the Literary Imagination*, New York: Vintage Books.

Pérez, D. (2014), "Ser Guaynabito," *Metro*, 5 March. https://www.metro.pr/pr/blogs/2014/03/05/opinion-guaynabito.html. Accessed on 15 January 2023.

Ramos-Zayas, A. Y. (2020), *Parenting Empires: Class, Whiteness, and the Moral Economy of Privilege in Latin America*, Durham: Duke University Press.

Rebollo-Gil, G. (2005), "Entre Cafres y Blanquitos: Perceptions of Race and Racism in Puerto Rico," PhD diss., College of Liberal Arts and Sciences, University of Florida, Gainesville. http://etd.fcla.edu/UF/UFE0012803/rebollogil_g.pdf. Accessed on 15 January 2023.

Rebollo-Gil, G. (2018), *Writing Puerto Rico: Our Decolonial Moment*, London: Palgrave Macmillan.

Redacción (2018), "Carlos Dávila Rinaldi Presenta su Nueva Obra en el Espacio Arte @ Plaza," *El Nuevo Día*, 10 June. https://www.magacin.com/eventos/fotogaleria/carlos-davila-rinaldi-presenta-su-nueva-obra-en-el-espacio-arte-at-plaza/#foto-1. Accessed on 15 January 2023.

Rekdal, P. (2021), *Appropriate: A Provocation*, New York: W.W. Norton.

Residente (2020), "René (Official video)," *YouTube*, 27 February. https://www.youtube.com/watch?v=O4f58BU_Hbs. Accessed on 15 January 2023.

Richardson, L. (1997), *Fields of Play: Constructing an Academic Life*, New Brunswick: Rutgers University Press.

Rivera Puig, M. (2018), "Darán Seguridad Privada en Condado," *El Vocero*. 21 August. https://www.elvocero.com/ley-y-orden/dar-n-seguridad-privada-en-condado/article_2e022af4-a4e0-11e8-b5bd-1392aa8aefc7.html. Accessed on 15 January 2023.

Rivera-Rideau, P. R. (2015), *Remixing Reggaetón: The Cultural Politics of Race in Puerto Rico*, Durham: Duke University Press.

Rivero, Y. M. (2005), *Tuning Out Blackness: Race and Nation in the History of Puerto Rican Television*, Durham: Duke University Press.

Robles, F., and P. Mazzei (2021), "Puerto Rico's Deposed Governor Describes His Family"s Panicked Flight from the Island," *New York Times*, 14 January. https://www.nytimes.com/2021/01/13/us/ricardo-rossello-puerto-rico.html. Accessed on 15 January 2023.

Rodríguez-Casellas, M. (2012), "Americano," *Revista Cruce*. http://www.revistacruce.com/new_revista/?q=americano. Accessed on 15 January 2023.

Rodríguez Juliá, E. (2011), "Blue Experts," *80grados*, 13 May. https://www.80grados.net/blue-experts/. Accessed on 15 January 2023.

Row, J. (2019), *White Flights: Race, Fiction and the American Imaginatio*, Minneapolis: Graywolf Press.

Russell Brown, K. (1996), "The Racial Hoax as Crime: The Law as Affirmation," *Indiana Law Journal* 71 (3): 594–621.

Salvo, J. M. (2020), *Reading Autoethnography: Reflections on Justice and Love*, New York: Routledge.

Schachter, J., and A. Bruce (2020), "Estimating Puerto Rico"s Population after María: Revising Methods to Better Reflect the Impact of Disaster," *United States Census Bureau*, 19 August. https://www.census.gov/library/stories/2020/08/est imating-puerto-rico-population-after-hurricane-maria.html. Accessed on 15 January 2023.

Segal, L. (2017), *Radical Happiness*, London: Verso.

Spocchia, G. (2021), "Puertorriqueños se Quejan de Turistas de EE.UU. por Desobedecer Reglas Impuestas por Pandemia," *Independent en Español* 20 March. https://www.independentespanol.com/noticias/turistas-estados-unidos-reg las-covid-puerto-rico-cubrebocas-b1820139.html. Accessed on 15 January 2023.

Sullivan, S. (2019), *White Privilege*, Cambridge: Polity Press.

Vidal-Ortiz, S. 2004), "On Being a White Person of Color: Using Autoethnography to Understand Puerto Ricans' Racialization," *Qualitative Sociology* 27 (2): 179–203.

Vilches Norat, V. (2018), *Geografías de lo Perdido*, San Juan: Ediciones Callejón.

Index

www.ingramcontent.com/pod-product-compliance
Lightning Source LLC
Chambersburg PA
CBHW062037270326

41929CB00014B/2463